Ivan Panin's Bible Chronology

In Three Parts

by

Ivan Panin

Ivan Panin

Edited by
Mark Vedder

Publishing Rights Reserved © 2017 by Mark Vedder. No part of this publication may be reproduced for publishing without written permission of the Editor or Publisher. Quotes are permitted with credit of this publication as source.

Library of Congress Control Number: 2017915759
Vedder, Mark 1965–
           Panin's Bible Chronology / Ivan Panin / Mark Vedder
              177 pp   cm
           Includes Prefaces
ISBN 978-1-941776-19-3
Historic Chronology of Scripture, Numeric Structure Explored

New England Bible Sales
262 Quaker Road
Sidney, Maine 04330
jptbooks@gmail.com
NewEnglandBibleSales.com
(207) 512-2636

                              2017
                    ISBN 978-1-941776-19-3
                 Publishing rights reserved
                                by
                          Mark Vedder
            sufferingduckman@gmail.com

CONTENTS

Preface to the 2017 Edition............................ 1
1950 Preface... 2

PART I

BIBLICAL CHRONOLOGY CANONS

I.	Point of view	3
II.	Present State of Bible Chronology	3
III.	Bible Canons	4
IV.	Canon I. The Bible alone is the Final Authority for its own Data.	4
V.	Canon II. The Old Testament text adopted as the basis of discussion is that of the Hebrew Masoretes, of the present Hebrew copies, of which the Protestant Versions are translations.	5
VI.	Canon III. The present Hebrew Text to be firmly held to, and abandoned only where a copyist's error is proved from the Bible itself; the correction, moreover, to be made only from the Bible itself.	6
VII.	Canon IV. A clear Statement in one part of the Bible is to be held to against others not so clear in other parts. The light from the clear to be thrown on the obscure, rather than the obscure to darken the light. A mere difficulty is not to annul a certainty.	13
VIII.	Canon V. The Terms of the original Bible Languages are to be strictly Adhered to in Translation: Keeping specially to the Distinction between Cardinal and Ordinal Numbers, and heeding the different Methods of using Chronological Terms.	15
IX.	Canon VI. The Dictionary Meaning of the Terms used is to be strictly Adhered to, and Departed from only when the ordinary Meaning is made Impossible by other Established Facts...	17
X.	Canon VII. The Reconciliation of what are apparently Discrepancies in the Bible Data must be along the Lines laid down in Canon I-VI; and any attempted Harmonisation on other lines stands Self-Condemned.	42
XI.	Canon VIII. In the Solution of Bible Difficulties	

	that which Covers an entire Class of Cases Stands as against those dealing with their individual Cases separately. The Simple Solution stands against the Complex.	44
XII.	Canon IX. In Matters Biblical the Notions of "Unlikely, Improbable, Hard to Believe, Incredible, Inconceivable," and their like, are not to be Entertained so as to make the Bible statements Void. Only what is demonstrably Irrational, or declared in the Bible itself to be Impossible, is to be allowed to Call in Question Bible Statements.	48

PART II

THE BIBLE DATA

The Bible Data	53
Years deducible from the Data of the Bible	58

Table I.
     Period 1. Adam to the Flood............ 125
     Period 2. Flood to Covenant............ 126
     Period 3. Covenant to Exodus......... 127
     Period 4. Exodus to Temple........... 128
     Period 5. Temple to Captivity......... 129
     Period 6. Captivity to Restoration.... 132
     Period 7. Restoration to the Christ... 133
     Period 8. Nativity to Pentecost........ 133
Table II.
     Kings of Israel and Judah................ 137

PART III

THE NUMERIC PHENOMENA

The Numeric Phenomena............................ 141
     Table III, The Eight Periods............ 143
     Table IV, Landmark Events............ 146
     Table V, Dates Derived from Genesis
               Alone...................... 158
     Table VI, Years Obtainable from
               Second Chronicles............... 167

Preface to the 2017 Edition

This is a word-for-word transcription of the 1950 edition of Panin's *Bible Chronology* edited by Gustav E. Hoyer. Mr. Hoyer's preface follows this one. We have kept the formatting as close as possible to that edition, and no changes of any kind were permitted in wording or punctuation.

Panin begins with nine *Canons* by which to approach chronology, providing an approach to the subject which is designed to eliminate useless debate.

His second section is a "List" of every knowable date in the Bible. This is a reference guide and is the core of the results of his years of research.

The third section is a guided tour through the undergirding of the numerics woven throughout the Chronology. While he could write volumes on the subject, he limits himself to clear examples that have specific impact.

The investigating researcher can rest assured that every divergence has been noted as such: there are no arbitrary corrections. Thus the archaic presentation style will make its presence felt; this gives as close as possible a sense of not only the content of his work, but the method.

The length of this book is deceptively short for the subject matter. However, the reader will find it concentrated and distilled, demanding one's full attention. The facts are detailed and internally consistent, the "Canons" are salient and would hold up in any academic court, and the numerics have their own distinct appeal.

Those familiar with the classic problems of chronology that are revisited by each generation of scholars will appreciate the depth of Panin's often unique approach.

—Mark Vedder, 2017

1950 Preface

Soon after his earliest discoveries of the numerical structure, or design, of the original Hebrew and Greek texts of the Bible, Mr. Ivan Panin began his research in the chronology of the Bible. In the year 1896 Mr. Panin published some of his findings in a publication of his own called "The Gospel of Christ," and these are found in the issues of January, February, and March. He further expounded the subject in a special publication, a periodical, called "Bible Numerics," in the issues of March-April, 1916, pp. 3-17 and May-June, pp 3-13 of the same year.

The first edition of *Bible Chronology* was printed for Mr. Panin in 1923 by the Armach Press, Toronto. The *Chronology* was reprinted in 1939, the reprint being made in Great Britain by Green & Co., Caxton Press, Lowestoft. After this reprint Mr. Panin commenced the work of correcting and revising the book for a second edition, but being overtaken by an illness which brought his ardent labours to an end, he was prevented from bringing his work on the *Chronology* to completion. It has thus become the duty of the present writer to continue the work of preparation for the press.

All matter extraneous to the subject has been eliminated in this edition; the word "Jehovah" is rendered "Lord" throughout the book; typographical errors have been corrected.

The book has been supplemented by an Index of Scripture Passages which will facilitate its use.

Results of future work of numerical analysis of passages in the Hebrew text which would necessitate corrections of any of the dates given in this book would not seriously affect the result in general.

The writer wishes to acknowledge the help received from the Rev. H. F. Schade in the work of revision, his assistance made it possible to present the book in this its second edition.

This new edition of Mr. Panin's great work, *Bible Chronology*, is sent forth in the name of our Lord and to His praise in the conviction that it will be a blessing to all who love God and find their delight in meditating on His Word.

GUSTAV. E. HOYER.

Chicago, July 1950

PART 1.
Bible Chronology Canons

I. POINT OF VIEW.

§ 1. The following pages are written in the conviction that the Bible has God for its author, a conviction amply justified by the facts brought forward in Part III of this work.

§ 2. As the book of God the only error the Bible may contain is that of copyist, printer, or translator. These once eliminated, every statement of the Bible must agree with every other. The harmony, however, is not always on the surface, is at times even deeply hid, but ever at last brought to light if reverently, diligently, and patiently sought. The Bible makes upon the reader certain inexorable demands. To those who comply it readily yields its secrets, treasures ere long, according to the capacity of each. To those who do not comply it abides sealed in proportion to their lack of compliance.

Only to the wise (but wise according to its standard: the childlike in temper, the poor in spirit, the lowly at heart) does it unfold itself: at first indeed as the book of wisdom, ere long also as the book of life, and last in all its majesty as the Book of God before which he may now indeed **tremble**, as at every other word of the living God, which is indeed like a hammer and like a fire: a hammer against all that is hard and proud; a fire against all that is only wood, hay, and stubble, however exalted in the sight of men.

II. PRESENT STATE OF BIBLE CHRONOLOGY.

§ 3. Through this book are scattered numerous chronological statements: but not all are readily reconcilable on the surface. Not a few, moreover, present real problems, solved only after long investigation. consideration, and prayer. On these problems, and even its plain statements, the ablest minds of Christendom have for centuries devoutly and faithfully toiled, yet with results far from satisfactory. To name if only among the moderns: Usher, Scaliger, Petavius, Newton, Prideaux, Ideler, Hales, Clinton, Browne, Jarvis, and the writers on Chronology in the various Bible Encyclopedias and dictionaries. No two among the dozens of writers entirely agree. On the central dates of the Flood, the Exodus, the 490 years of Daniel, some are even centuries apart.

§ 4. It was the writer's belief that order can be brought out of this chaos; and this he believes is accomplished in Part II. That he **has** succeeded is demonstrated in Part III. When a conglomeration of fragments of diverse shapes and sizes is at last put together so that each fragment fits into its neighbour, and there thus appears an artist's figure hitherto unsuspected—the figure itself becomes its own evidence. Accordingly in Part III Bible Chronology is found to be not a mere collection of fragments with some lone unifying thread running through it (which hitherto has been the most that could be expected by even the best friends of the Bible), but a gigantic Figure, wrought out to the minutest detail with the consummate art of all hitherto unheard-of Genius.

III. BIBLE CANONS.

§ 5. The confusion noted above, prevailing widely not only in Bible Chronology but in all matters biblical, is largely due to the failure to give heed to certain canons which from its very nature as God's book the Bible imposes on all who have to do therewith as other than mere merchandise. Confusion, discord about its purpose and meaning, is the penalty it exacts from those who from whatever cause go contrary to the laws peculiarly its own. Accordingly, in this work the following principles have been strictly held to:

IV. CANON I.

The Bible alone is the Final Authority for its own Data.

§ 6. This canon is necessitated by the acceptance of the Bible as God's Book. Its own verdict as to the temper with which it is to be approached is: "Thus saith the Lord . . . to this man will I look, to him that is poor and of contrite spirit, and that **trembleth at My word**" (Isa. 66: 1—2). As God's Book, as it brooks no suspicion, so neither does it court endorsements, testimonials, or letters of commendation from historians, monuments, tablets, coins, and the various other indispensable materials of Profane Chronology. This canon accordingly fixes the exact relation between the Bible and other sources of information in matters chronological.

§ 7. The other sources may indeed be used to clear up obscurities, or to strengthen interpretations that need strengthening; they may even be used as witnesses before those unfortunate enough to require a witness unto God's book (and even this as mere condescension, in nowise is aught due to such): as helps, in short, they can only be welcomed; but they must in nowise be allowed to assume authority as against the Bible. If other authorities agree therewith, so much the better for them; if they disagree, it may well give occasion to examine the biblical data whether they really do state what they apparently state, whether they have been understood as they should be understood; the disagreement may even be a reason for holding the biblical data in abeyance for a while till perchance the disagreement be at last harmonised or eliminated; but further than this the disagreement on the part of other sources must not be allowed to go.

§ 8. Adherence to this canon thus settles at the start the true relation between the Bible and (to take as an example the case most favourable to disagreement with the Bible) the Ptolemy Canon, to which the Bible has been made to bend even by its professed friends. This work is declared as of the highest authority by the best judges, and this truly enough if it be added: but only within certain limits. For a certain period of Bible history this work is the only profane chronological authority, No **contradiction** has yet been established between it and the Bible, but neither has any harmony. Accordingly nearly all the conservative, Bible chronologers accept Ptolemy as the standard, and unbendingly bend the Bible thereto: with result not only of distortion of the Bible, but also dismal confusion of history as well as chronology.

Now Canon I assigns Ptolemy his proper place: it does not diminish his worth, not even reduce his rank. Where prince before, he may still remain prince, but before the Bible he is only a prince in presence of his—Sovereign.

And what is true of Ptolemy's Canon is equally true of every other source of knowledge in fields covered also by the Bible. This is especially true of much that in these days likes to think of itself as Science. In its own legitimate field it is indeed supreme, though even there it is already presumption, which are long becomes downright arrogance, to assert that because things have been **thus** during the few millennia within the experience of man, they always have been and always will continue thus. But whenever Science professes to contradict the Bible in **its** field, it proves itself by this very fact to be either No-Science, or at best only dyspeptic science.

V. CANON II

The Old Testament text adopted as the basis of discussion is that of the Hebrew Masoretes, of the present Hebrew copies, of which the Protestant Versions are translations.

§ 9. For a Bible Chronology there are four rivals in the field as authorities: the Hebrew Masoretic text, its Greek translation by the Seventy, the Samaritan Five Books of Moses, and Josephus. Each presents a different chronology, with a difference in some data of a thousand years between them. Josephus drops out at once from the competition, as one who had before him no more than the same three rivals that we have. Josephus is a mere interpreter of other authorities, not an original authority himself for Bible dates. The state of his text in matters of dates is moreover such as to prevent the construction of a consistent system of chronology thereon as yet.

§ 10. Of the preservation and transmission of the Samaritan text next to nothing is known. There are no materials for deciding on its claims as rival of the Hebrew and the Greek. It agrees wholly with neither. Enough suspicion, moreover, has already been thrown upon it by Gesenius as to absolve the student for the present from taking seriously its chronological claims as against the Hebrew and the Seventy.

§ 11. The Seventy is a translation only, with now and then an addition to the Hebrew. Its transmission, therefore, was not watched over as zealously, or even as carefully, as that of the original. The Hebrew was always held by its custodians the Jews as their final authority. It was its divisions, chapters, verses, words, and letters that were so carefully counted and recorded. It was its manner of being copied and handled that was so carefully protected by the various stringent rules about pen, ink, and parchment and scribe, length of page, line, and spacings. And the Hebrew, moreover, is in possession of the field. The burden of proof is on its rivals to show cause why it should be ousted and they installed. This proof after a battle of decades between the acutest intellects of Christendom has not been produced.

VI. CANON III.

The present Hebrew Text to be firmly held to, and abandoned only where a copyist's error is proved from the Bible itself; the correction, moreover, to be made only from the Bible itself.

§ 12. Thus 1 Kings 6: 1 is in the Hebrew literally: "And it was in the year eighty and year four hundreds from Israel's children's departure from Egypt land, in the year the fourth, in month Ziph (that is the month the second) of Solomon's reign over Israel—and he built the house unto the Lord."

The simple English is: 480 years from the Exodus, in the second month of

Year Four of his reign Solomon began build the Temple.

Three peculiar but usual idioms of the Hebrew are to be noted here: (1) the numbers are given not in the letters of the alphabet (corresponding somewhat to the modern Arabic figures), but in their own names, words in full **eighty** and four **hundreds**, not 480, nor even 80 and 400. (2) The word year is repeated: not 480 years, but 80 years and 400 years. (3) The word **year**, though plural with numbers up to ten, is singular with numbers above ten. Hence it is not 80 years and 400 years, but 80 year and 400 year, necessitating a transposition of the number in the English, which perhaps varies somewhat the sense of the phrase in the original.

§ 13. With these **facts** before us we are confronted with the assertion of all the advocates of a longer period between the Exodus and the Temple that 480 is an error, and they make it therefore 580.

As the year of the Temple is a cardinal date for Bible chronology, and its proper placing is a good illustration of both the need and soundness of this canon, it is best discussed at some length.

§ 14. Four plausible reasons are brought forth in favour of the notion that there is an "error" here.

(1) Hebrew letters being used for numerals (like our Arabic figures), one letter is readily mistaken for another where there is some resemblance between them, so that the letter for 10 might be mistaken for the letter for 6; or 8 for 5, or 4 for 200, etc.

(2) Josephus makes this period **nearly** 580 years.

(3) The book of Judges requires at least 580 years for this period.

(4) Paul's statement in Acts 13: 17—21 requires a longer period than 480 years.

As to (1). Neither in the Hebrew Old Testament nor the Greek New Testament are **letters** ever used for numerals. The words for the numbers are always given. Four, not 4. Hundred, not 100. If **chamishi**, five, can be mistaken into **arbaah**, four, it can be mistaken into any other number, and 680, 780, or 980 are as likely as 580.

§ 15. As to (2). However trustworthy Josephus be as to FACTS he personally testifies to, in relation to the status of the Hebrew text of the Old Testament the mention of his name is irrelevant. He nowhere discusses the Hebrew text. The status, moreover, of his own Greek text is such that the contradictions therein in matters chronological are best accounted for by the need of much revision of his text which has apparently suffered not a little from transcribers, editors, or harmonizers.

Moreover, the numbers of Josephus for this period are 612 in one place and 592 in another. The change of the biblical 480 into 580 is thus of no help here toward agreement with Josephus at any rate.

§ 16. As to (3). The data of Judges, interpreted in favour of the longer chronology, **and only thus**, require for this period not 520, but some 630 years.

As to (4). The data of Paul in Acts 13:17—21, interpreted likewise in favour of the longer period, but only thus, call not for 580, but for some **nine hundred** years.

All the advocates of the longer chronology agree in rejecting, against all the manuscripts, the number 480 in 1 Kings 6: 1, but no two agree as to the exact length of the individual items of this period: each writer having for these a scheme of his own to harmonize it with the preconceptions already brought thereto. They agree, however, that the number is "probably" 580, but produce no **textual** authority for it; no manuscripts, no versions. The only version here that speaks, the Seventy, is indeed against the 480, but its number is not more, but less—440.

The violence thus done to the Hebrew text in substituting from mere conjecture 580 for 480 is not only arbitrary and contrary to all the duties one owes to ancient documents, to say nothing of the persons who wrote them (the golden rule having been promulgated in favour of the dead as well as of the living), it fails even of its purpose: since 580 serves here no better than 480. The "discrepancy" between Judges and Acts on the one side and Kings on the other is left. The so-called error might as well have been any number other than 480.

§ 17. The **apparent** discrepancy noted above is a difficulty: be duly recognized explained and harmonized; but it does not justify on the grounds given above the abandonment of the Hebrew text. In matters scientific, above all in matters biblical, the procedure of the school boy, who rubs out the figures when they do not add together correctly and substitutes others, is in nowise to be imitated, least of all in an age that boasts of a better equipment for the discovery, or even pursuit of truth than any other. This departure from the text has not settled Bible chronology; it has only thrown it into confusion, as is testified to by the failure of any two of the Longer chronologists to agree as to the details of this period.

It is as a safeguard against the numerous occasions for confusion, of which the case of the 480 years is only a notable example, that Canon III is to be adhered to.

§ 18. As this case of the 480 years is a good example not only of the need of this canon but also of its efficacy, the demonstration is herewith given from the book of Judges itself that at least one statement of his own demands a shorter period than is apparently demanded by its data as a whole.

For its sins the people of God are in Judg. 10: 6—11: 28, delivered into the hand of Ammon for eighteen years. They repent, and Jephthah is raised up to deliver them. He sends to Ammon to inquire why he is fighting his people. The answer is, "Because when he came up from Egypt Israel took away my land from Arnon even unto Jabbok and unto Jordan. Now, therefore, restore those again in peace" (Judg. 11: 13). Jephthah answers that the land had not been taken from Ammon, but from the Amorites. Ammon therefore has no claim upon them; and then adds, While Israel dwelt in Heshbon and her towns, and in Aroer and her towns, and in all the cities by the side of Arnon, three hundred years, wherefore did ye not recover them within that time? (Judg. 11: 26).

§ 19. From the possession, therefore, of Heshbon to the end of the Ammon oppression is thus according to Jephthah 300 years.

When these began is readily made out thus:

(1) Aaron the priest, in Numb. 33: 38, went up into Mount Hor at the Lord's command and "died there in years forty from the departure of the children of Israel from Egypt land, in the fifth month, on [day] one of the month." (2) After mourning for Aaron at Mount Hor (Numb. 21: 4) thirty days (Numb. 20: 29) the children of Israel journey from Mount Hor by way to the Red Sea to compass Edom land. Shortly after (Numb. 21: 24-25) "Israel smote him [Sihon the Amorite king] with the edge of the sword, and

possessed his land from Arnon unto Jabbok . . . And Israel dwelt in all the cities of the Amorites, in Heshbon and all its towns."

These 300 years then began in year 40 from the Exodus, and ended with year 18 of the Ammon oppression.

§ 20. The data for this period from Judges are twelve in number, as follows:

1.	3: 8	Israel is delivered for their sins to Cushan Rishathaim	years 8.
2.	3: 11	They repent and are delivered through Othniel	years 40.
3.	3: 14	Sin again. Eglon oppression follows	years 18.
4.	3: 30	Deliverance through Ehud	years 80.
5.	4: 3	Oppression by Jabin	years 20.
6.	5: 31	Deliverance through Barak	years 40.
7.	6: 1	Midian Oppresses	years 7.
8.	8: 28	Deliverance through Gideon	years 40.
9.	9: 22	Abimelech reigns	years 3.
10.	10: 2	Tola judge,	years 23.
11.	10: 3	Jair judge,	years 22.
12.	10: 8	Ammon oppression	years 18.

The sum of these twelve data is 319 years. To these are to be added: (1) the six years from the end of the forty in the wilderness to the division of the land; (2) the time from the division of the land to the first oppression, which, as shown in Part II at year 2610 is 27 years. This makes the time from Heshbon to the end of the Ammon oppression 352 years. Jephthah says only 300. The twelve data given above cannot therefore mean to cover 52 years more. The difficulty moreover is not removed by calling 300 a round number. Round numbers, as shown below, are ruled out by Canon VI, and are to be admitted only where demonstrated as such. Here, however, it is not only undemonstrated, it is out of question. 352 is nearer 400 than 300; and Jephthah would have been a poor pleader of his cause to name 300 when 400 would have been not only nearer the truth, but would have served his purpose better. If a round number were at all to be used here, no reason can be given why 300 or even 400 should be used rather than the obvious 350.

Judges itself thus furnishes a check of its own upon its chronology, and thus warns us not to receive all its data as material for a **consecutive** chronology, since up to the end of the 300 years it is already, if consecutive, 52 years out of the way according to a datum of its own.

So far, therefore, as Judges is concerned the 480 years from the Exodus to the Temple need not yet be disturbed. And as the chronology of Acts 13: 19 is apparently linked with it, whatever clears up the one clears up also the other. The calling in question, therefore, of the number 480 on the authority of Judges and Acts is not yet warranted by what has so far been brought forward.

§ 21. Again: In 2 Kings 24: 8, Jehoiachin "was a son of eighteen years at his reigning, and he reigned in Jerusalem three months." In 2 Chron. 36: 9 he is a son of **eight** years at his reigning, and he reigned three mouths and ten days. All the manuscripts and versions retain the eight here. It is a singular testimony to the fidelity of the Hebrew custodians of the text that this apparent discrepancy is left without a trace of attempt at correction.

The commentators, however, are all here at one. If ever, they say, there was a textual error it is surely here. The king was either 18 or 8, he could not have been both. No room here for harmonizings, allegorizings, deeper meanings. An error here surely is, and moreover it is in Chronicles. For in the other book the Babylon king carried away Jehoiachin to Babylon, and the mother of the king, and the **wives** of the king. At 18 he might have a wife, and even wives, but not at 8, at least not more than the one to whom he might have been betrothed even at that early age. And even for this latter assumption there is no occasion in view of the rival 18 in the other book. A textual error is here therefore uniformly accepted by all. Read 18 for 8. Lovers of the Bible charge indeed the error only to the original scribe. But enemies of the Bible are content with nothing short of an error by the author himself.

§ 22. Now here it is where Canon III demands heed. A difficulty here certainly is, but one in nowise compelling enough to justify violence to the author. Such drastically might perhaps be tolerated in an ordinary book, but not in the book of God. The ways of God are not as the ways of man, neither is His Book as the book of a man. It is still possible that the father found it advisable to appoint his son fellow-ruler even at the age of eight, The circumstances of his reign do not preclude it, would even justify it. As such a co-reign is not infrequent in Israel, and is found at least once in the southern kingdom, no one has a right to eliminate here a co-reign of father and son as an impossibility. "Not credible," "improbable," "unlikely," "strange," are all irrelevant here. Folk living thousands of years as well as miles from certain events are not the most fitted to say off hand what at such vast distance of time, place, and circumstance is possible or impossible, likely or unlikely.

§ 23. But even a glance at the Hebrew should have halted commentators here, for the error, if any, covers the word **year** as well as the numeral 8. It is plural here, as is usual with numbers up to ten, whereas with 18 it would be singular. This so-called error is thus not merely casual, it is studied, meditated error, all the more so since in Chronicles the ten days not mentioned in Kings are carefully added to the three months of that reign. This Latter circumstance alone should have protected here the sacred writer from the habitual criticism dealt out to him so rashly by the two writers of the Hastings Bible dictionary.

With this co-reign thus possible Canon III forbids the disregard thereof. Of the two evils, the tampering with the text on grounds short of demonstration, and the admission of an unproven, and even unmotived but possible co-reign, the latter is not only by far the smaller, but the choice thereof extends so the dead at least that fairness which is extended to the living by these for whom the Golden Rule is still aught more than mere rhetoric.

§ 24. Other is indeed the case of 2 Chron. 16: 1, "In year thirty and six of Asa's reign Baasha king of Israel went up against Judah and built Ramah." Here Baasha is alive and vigorous in 36 Asa. But in 1 Kings 15: 33 the account is year three of Asa . . . Baasha . . . reigned over all Israel in Tirzah—twenty and four year years." In I Kings 16: 8 it is, In year twenty and six of Asa . . . Elah son of Baasha reigned in Tirzah—two years. The twenty-four current years of Baasha are thus accounted for. 1 Baasha being 3 Asa, 24 Baasha is 26 Asa; and Elah son of Baasha duly begins his reign in that year. He reign, moreover, after the death of his father; for in 1 Kings 16: 6 Baasha slept with his fathers, and was buried in Tirzah, and Elah his son reigned **in his stead**. In 26 Asa then Baasha is dead according to Kings, but according to Chronicles he was still warring against Judah and building a fortress ten years later. The text of Kings is thus consistent throughout, it is Chronicles that perplexes. All attempts to harmonize Kings and Chronicles here are at best only plausible, if indeed the remedy offered is not at times as bad as the disease. Thus Archbishop Usher, followed here by Bishop Patrick, Adam Clarke, and others, holds that by "year thirty and six of Asa's reign," (or **kingdom** as **Malcuth** may also mean) is meant year 36 of the kingdom of **Judah**, which began with Rehoboam in 3054 from Adam. This would be 16 Asa, or 3089 Adam, where Baasha's attempt on Ramah may indeed fit in.

12

This explanation is, of course, not absolutely impossible. But here again the choice is between two evils: a possible copyist's error in the text, or a novel, unique interpretation of a common phrase habitually used only in the one technical sense. An interpretation which, moreover, offers no compensation for the violence it does to both Dictionary and common sense.

Accordingly, here the writer, with all his veneration for Usher and Patrick, and respect for Adam Clarke, is ready to admit a primitive copyist's error (all the more so as the number 36 is demonstrated in Part III to be impossible). But as the Bible itself furnishes no means for correction here, the passage according to Canon III is left for the present as it is, until in the goodness of God the means for correction are at hand.

VII. CANON IV.

A clear Statement in one part of the Bible is to be held to against others not so clear in other parts. The light from the clear to be thrown on the obscure, rather than the obscure to darken the light. A mere difficulty is not to annul a certainty.

§ 25. The case of 1 Kings with the 480 years from Exodus to Temple, which as already seen fails under Canon III, fails also under this Canon IV. The statement in Kings is clear. The data of Judges and Acts in apparent conflict therewith are acknowledged by all to need elucidation. Accordingly Kings in this case is to be used for clearing up Judges and Acts rather than letting their obscurity darken the light of Kings.

§ 26. Likewise in Gal. 3: 16—18 "the promises were spoken to Abraham . . . But this I say: A covenant confirmed afore by God the Law which came **four hundred and thirty years after**, disannulleth not unto the voiding of the promise. For if the inheritance is of law, it is no longer of promise. But to Abraham God hath granted it by promise." This statement through Paul is clear and positive. From the Covenant with Abraham (whenever it was) to the Law (given at Sinai) is 430 years. But by the side of this is Ex. 12: 40—41: "And the sojourning of Israel's sons who sojourned in Egypt had was thirty years and four hundred years. And it was at the end of thirty years and four hundred years (and it was the self-same day) that all the hosts of the Lord went out from Egypt land."

As this was only some three months from the Law at Sinai ("In the third month after Israel's sons were gone forth from Egypt land, the same day they came into the Sinai wilderness"—Ex. 19:1), Gal 3: 16 is here apparently contradicted: seemingly this passage asserts that from the going down of the sons of Jacob with their father to sojourn in Egypt to the Law it was 430 years. But the Covenant with Abraham was at the latest the year before Isaac was born, when Abraham was ninety-nine. Isaac was 60 when Jacob was born, and Jacob was 130 when he came to Egypt. But year, 60, 130, and 430 years, give 621 years from the (Covenant to the Law, if the data of Exodus are correctly understood here.

§ 27. Galatians is clear, Exodus not so clear. "Sojourned," "Israel's sons" (apparently including the father also), "Egypt land" to which the regions of Abraham's and Isaac's abode may have been subject some time in their day) —every one of these terms needs much elucidation before they can be allowed to annul the clear statement in Galatians. Canon IV. thus makes Galatians the standard here by which Exodus is to be interpreted, rather than Exodus for Galatians; the clear is standard for the obscure, not the obscure for the clear: Exodus meanwhile being held in abeyance for further light thereon from elsewhere.

§ 28. Subject to the same Canon is the manner of establishing the year of Abraham's birth, which affects all succeeding Bible dates. In Acts 7: 2—4 the statement through Stephen is clear that when Abraham left Haran his father Terah was—dead. "The God of the Glory appeared to our father Abraham . . . and said to him, Come out of thy land . . . Then came he out of the Chaldeans' land and dwelt in Haran; and thence **after his father's death** [God] removed him into this land wherein ye now dwell." In Gen. 11: 32 "all the days of Terah were five years and two hundred years." In Gen. 12: 4 Abraham is a "son of five years and seventy years when he departed from Haran." According then to Stephen, expressly said to have been then "filled with Holy Spirit," Terah was 205 years less 75 when Abraham was born, or 130; and this statement is clear and simple. But in Gen. 11: 26 "Terah lived seventy years, and begat Abram,. Nahor, and Haran," apparently begetting triplets then of whom Abraham is the first-born. In the clear light of Acts 7: 2 —4 this statement at once demands elucidation. If Abraham was born when his father was 70, he was at Terah's death 135, not 75. Canon IV. here accordingly requires that the clear statement through Stephen be held to against Gen. 11: 26, where there is room for the meaning that Terah became a father at 70; and his children were Abram, Nahor, and Haran: of whom the first is not necessarily the oldest, but named first for an obvious reason, though not given here. With this and like possibilities Gen. 11: 26 can with propriety be held in abeyance for further light, with Stephen, however, meanwhile as the standard. This all the more since the case of Abram, Nahor and Haran is paralleled by that of Shem, Ham and Japhet, where is **demonstrated** that Shem, though named first, was not only not the oldest of triplets, but was two years younger than Japhet.

VIII. CANON V.

The Terms of the original Bible Languages are to be strictly Adhered to in Translation. Keeping specially to the Distinction between Cardinal and Ordinal Numbers, and heeding the different Methods of using Chronological Terms.

§ 29. Thus in Gen. 7: 6 "Noah was a son of six hundred years, and the flood of waters was on the earth." This and all like cases is rendered in the English version 600 years **old**. On its face the precise meaning of the chronological term "a son of years" may indeed need clearing up. It may or may not mean that Noah had already lived full 600 years. But the English here is at least not a mistranslation. When however they render Gen. 7: 11, "In the six hundredth year of Noah's life." making Noah live up to that time only 599 years, they mistranslate. For the Hebrew has it: "In year six hundred years." This peculiar expression "**In year six hundred years**," whatever else it may mean, does not mean the six hundred**th year**. It was meant in fact to guard against this very error. For the whole verse is: "in year six hundred of Noah's life, in the second month, on day seventeen of the month, on this day all fountains of a great deep were broken up, and windows of the heavens were opened." Whatever the reason, a distinction between the month on the one hand, and the day and the year on the other, is kept up: Year six hundred, day seventeen, but **second** month, not month two.

Likewise in Gen. 8:13: "And it was in year one and six hundred of Noah, in the first [month], on [day] one of the month." Year 601, day one, but **first** month.

§ 30. The same distinction is oft kept up elsewhere. In 1 Kings 6: 1, as seen in § 12, it is carefully made between the cardinal and ordinal numbers. The English translations have it: "And it came to pass in the four hundred and eight**ieth** year," thus making the full period from Exodus to Temple 479 years, shortening the chronology here by one year, and in the case of the Flood by another year in the same manner. The Hebrew gives Solomon's regnal year as an ordinal, "the fourth"; but the period as a cardinal number: "eighty years and four hundred years"—the very distinction being designed to warn against mistake.

The habitual disregard of these distinctions by Bible chronologers in the numerous data of Kings and Chronicles has made of the whole simple chronology of this period a veritable jungle at their hands, through which the way to daylight can be cut only by means of anarchies, interregna, or joint reigns not found in the Bible.

§ 31. How softly one has to tread in the presence of the utmost accuracy of Scripture in the original is best seen from an example or two. Of the ten pre-flood patriarchs Adam is the first and Noah the last. These two have accordingly their years given thus: "And all the days that Adam lived were nine hundred years and thirty years." "And all the days that Noah lived were nine hundred years and fifty years" (Gen. 5: 3—31; 9: 29). The hundreds are in these two cases given first. But for the eight patriarchs between the first and last it is: "And all the days of Seth were twelve years and nine hundred years," with the hundreds not first but last in every case.

§ 32. In Ex. 6: 16, 18, 20, the years of the lives of Levi, Kohath and Amram are given respectively as "seven and thirty and hundred years," "three and thirty and hundred years," and "seven and thirty and hundred years." Years is given only once; and the order is: units, tens, hundreds. But the lives of Sarah, Abraham and Ishmael are given thus: "And Sarah's life was hundred years and twenty years and seven years—years of Sarah's life." "And these [are the] days of Abraham's life which he lived: hundred years and seventy years and five years." "And these [the] years of Ishmael's life: hundred years, thirty years and seven years" (Gen. 23: 1; 25: 7, 17). Here **year** is repeated thrice, with each denomination; and the denominations, moreover, are reversed from the order of Levi. Kohath and Amram. Here the order is: hundreds, tens, units. Of Isaac it is: "And Isaac's days were hundred years and eighty years' (Gen. 35: 28), which in the absence of units still holds to the manner and order of his father, mother and brother. But with Jacob it is: "And Jacob's days were, the years of his life, seven years and forty and hundred year; (Gen. 47: 28). Here the order is the same with Levi, Kohath, and Amram; units first, hundreds last. The repetition of year is kept, but only once instead of twice; so that the case of Jacob is midway between Abraham, Sarah and Ishmael, with their **year** thrice, and Levi, Kohath and Amram with their one.

The reason for these changes in the notation of the length of life, and others like them, are unknown to the writer. But a dull reader indeed would he be of **God's** book, if he were take all this as mattering naught, unimportant. meaningless . . .

IX. CANON VI.

The Dictionary Meaning of the Terms used is to be strictly Adhered to, and Departed from only when the ordinary Meaning is made Impossible by other Established Facts.

§ 33. The disregard of this Canon by all Bible Chronologers in at least two crucial data has completely deranged not only the Bible chronology, but also all chronology after 2083 from Adam: since Profane Chronology is based on the synchronisms of some years of Nebuchadnezzar of Babylon with those of Jehoiakim and Zedekiah of Judah. These two dates best illustrate the utmost need of this Canon:

§ 34. In Gal. 3: 17 Paul says: "A covenant confirmed afore by God, the Law which came four hundred and thirty years after, doth not disannul." This statement makes two demands upon the correct locating of its dates upon the chart: (1) The 430 years must begin with a COVENANT, with nothing short thereof; not with something like it, or even near it. It must be a **covenant**. (2) The period from this Covenant to the Law must be **four hundred and thirty years**, and not merely "about" that number, nor any other number. It must be just what Paul says: 430. Moreover, Ex. 12: 41 says expressly, "It was at [the] end of thirty years and four hundred years,—and it was on that very day, that all hosts of the Lord went out from Egypt land." The 430 years, from the time they began at the Covenant, apparently ended **to a day** at the Exodus. Not only 430 years, but 430 years **exactly**.

§ 35. In spite, however, of these two explicit requirements, these 430 years are dated by chronologers with one accord, so far as is known to the writer, from what is designated as Abraham's Call, when he was seventy-five, in 2083 from Adam. This event is told in Gen. 12: 1—4, 7, 9, thus:

"And the Lord said to Abram, Get thee out of thy country, and from thy kindred, and from thy father's house unto the land that I will show thee, and I will make thee a great nation, and will bless thee and make thy name great, and be thou a blessing. And I will bless them that bless thee, and him that curseth thee I will curse, and in thee shall all the families of the earth be blessed. And Abram went as the Lord had spoken unto him, and Lot went with him. And Abram was a son of five years and seventy years when he departed from Haran . . . . And the Lord appeared to Abram and said, Unto thy seed will l give this land; and there he built an altar unto the Lord who appeared unto him. And he removed thence to the mountain on the east of Bethel, and pitched his tent having Bethel on the west and Ai on the east; and there he built an altar to the Lord, and called upon the name of the Lord. And Abram journeyed, going on still toward the South."

§ 36. Here is indeed the Lord's call unto Abram, the date also is there: Abram is seventy-five; and he obtains additional promises in answer to his obedience. But **there is here no** COVENANT. A gracious call from the Lord, the promise of reward for obedience, Abram's obedience, and the consequent enlargement of the first promise, are indeed all here, and duly dated, but the vital requisite of the **Covenant** is not here. The 430 from the Covenant cannot therefore begin when Abram was 75 in 2083, when no covenant with him is recorded.

Thus every Chronology based on 2083 as the Covenant year at once—collapses.

§ 37. No covenant with Abram is mentioned till Gen. 15: 18, but this is some time after the Call.

In Gen. 12:1-8 Abram at 75 leaves Haran, goes to Canaan hundreds of miles off, leaves it only because of famine, and goes to Egypt, another long distance. Sarah is long enough in Pharaoh's house to be the cause of his being plagued by the Lord with great plagues, himself and his house (Gen. 12: 10—20). Abram leaves Egypt with "sheep and oxen and he-asses and men servants and maid servants and she-asses and camels." Thus encumbered, in days when fifteen miles a day was good progress, he gets back to Bethel. There is difficulty about pasture for the herds, and Lot parts from him for Sodom. There is war between Sodom and its allies, and Chederlaomer and his: five kings against four; and Lot is taken with the king of Sodom. Abram pursues, and delivers his nephew. It is **after** all this that "the word of the Lord came to Abram in a vision," which ended in a covenant. "On that day the Lord made a covenant with Abram, saying: Unto thy seed have I given this land, from Egypt's river to the great river, the river Euphrates" (Gen. 15: 18).

§ 38. This might well be the Covenant required, since shortly after the Call the promise had been merely, To thy seed will I give this land. Now it is, I have given. Hitherto the promise had been conditional, depending on his obedience, faithfulness. Now it is made sure (have given, henceforth stablished, irrevocable), because a Covenant has now been made between the contracting parties, and duly ratified with sacrifices on Abram's part, and the flaming torch passing between the pieces on the Lord's part. "When the sun went down and it was dark, behold a smoking furnace and a flaming torch that passed between the pieces."

It was in connection moreover with this covenant that "Abram believed God, and it was reckoned to him for righteousness." It is with this faith in the promised Seed in whom all the nations were to be blessed, with this faith in the Lamb of God which taketh away the sins of the world, it is with this evangelical faith that Abram became, according to Rom. 4: 11, father of the faithful of all the succeeding ages. A covenant, a most important covenant, is thus indeed made here with Abram; but this covenant, which thus meets all the other requirements, fails in the one essential for Chronology: it is not—dated. The time occupied by the events of Gen. 12: 10 to 15: 2 cannot be determined. The only event dated is the war between the five kings and the four; and even this only that it began in year thirteen of Chedarlaomer (Gen. 14: 1—5). But when this king began to reign is not stated.

§ 39. The next event recorded after this covenant is in Gen. 16: 1—3, where Sarai gives Hagar to Abram for a wife; this is "after Abram had dwelt ten years in Canaan land" (verse 3). What is known of this covenant, therefore, is that it took place at least a year after Abram left Haran at 75 (if not several years), but not later than Abram's year 85, since he begat Ishmael at 86. But this leaves the Covenant from which the 430 years are to be dated undetermined, with a possible variation of several years for its limits.

This failure to meet the one essential requirement for establishing its date is fatal to the claim of this covenant being the one needed. And the entire Bible Chronology, once the beginning of the 430 years being left obscure, with the Profane Chronology linked thereto, is after 2083 from Adam, left in suspense, a bridge with one end short of the shore.

As, therefore, the dating of the 430 years from the Call of Abram at 75 is a violation of Canon VI, so also is the same dating from this Covenant. The one is no covenant, the other has no date.

§ 40. Far other is the case with Gen. 17: 1—27. In the very first verse of this account of the Covenant as if a bell is rung, lest the date be missed by the careless. "And Abram (he is still Abram, not yet the covenanted with Abraham) was a son of ninety years and nine years; and the Lord appeared to

Abram and said to him: I am God Almighty, walk before Me, and be perfect; and I will **make My covenant** (no longer a covenant) between Me and thee, and will multiply thee exceedingly. And Abram fell on his face, and God talked with him, saying: As for Me, behold **My Covenant is with thee,** and thou shalt be father of a multitude of nations. Neither shall thy name be called Abram any more, but thy name shall be called Abraham, for I have made thee father of a multitude of nations . . . And I will stablish **My Covenant between Me and thee and thy seed after thee** throughout their generations for an ETERNAL COVENANT to be God unto thee and thy seed after thee . . . **As for thee, thou shalt keep My Covenant: thou and thy seed after thee** throughout their generations. THIS IS MY COVENANT: WHICH YE SHALL KEEP BETWEEN ME AND YOU AND THY SEED AFTER THEE. EVERY MALE AMONG YOU SHALL BE CIRCUMCISED. And ye shall be circumcised in the flesh of your foreskin, and it shall be a token of a covenant between Me and you . . . **And the uncircumcised male who is not circumcised in the flesh of his foreskin, that soul shall be cut off from his people, he hath broken My covenant.** . . . And Abraham was a son of ninety and nine years when he was circumcised in the flesh of his foreskin; and Ishmael was a son of thirteen years when he was circumcised."

§ 41. Of the several chimes with which this covenant is rung in three are chronological. In verse 1 Abram is 99; in verse 20 Abraham, now circumcised, is 99; and in verse 25 Ishmael is thirteen, he having been born when Abraham was 86 (Gen. 16: 16). In verse 2 the covenant is only promised. In verse 3 Abraham responds with humiliation and Worship. This the Lord honours with the assurance that the covenant hitherto only promised now is with him. (verse 4), and now gives him the new, covenant name Abraham (verse 5). But this as yet only his personal covenant. To be enlarged to his seed also, the covenant must be ratified by Abraham himself and his seed after him by a definite act of obedience, circumcision. And as no uncircumcised were within the covenant, being cut off, this covenant with Abraham was not in effect till himself and his put their signature, seal thereto upon their flesh. The covenant thus ratified by both parties now becomes valid, and the promised heir of the Covenant is then and there named, and is duly born next year. "THIS IS MY COVENANT which ye shalt keep" (verse 10). This is the covenant duly signed, duly ratified, and **duly dated**, by both parties: by God in giving Abraham the new name, and in opening Sarah's womb; and by Abraham in his obedience for himself and his house by circumcision. This is thus the only covenant from which Paul could date the 430 years to the Law: the one made with Abraham when he was 99, in 2107 ($7 \times 7 \times 43$, three and four being also seven) from Adam.

§ 42. A like violation of Canon V in the received dates of the Babylon captivity period results in the same confusion for all the dates thereafter. Chronologers are nearly unanimous in dating the Seventy Years' captivity of Judah from 4 Jehoiakim, in 3428, a year which meets neither of the two specifications conditioning this period:

(1) In Dan. 9: 1—2 it is: "In year one of Darius, son of Ahasuerus, . . . in year one of his reign I Daniel understood by books the number of the years whereof the word of the Lord came to Jeremiah the prophet for accomplishing desolations of Jerusalem—seventy years." Here, as in the case of the Covenant, two specifications must be complied with: (1) Jerusalem must be DESOLATE for (2) seventy years; any state of Jerusalem short of desolation thus failing to meet the need.

§ 43. Daniel only refers to Jeremiah, and these are the passages he refers to:

(2) Jer. 25: 9—12. "Behold, I will send and take all the families of the North, and unto Nebuchadnezzar king of Babylon My servant, and will bring them against this land and against its inhabitants, and against all these nations round about, and I will utterly destroy them, and make them an astonishment and a hissing and perpetual desolations. . . . This whole land shall be desolation and astonishment, and these nations shall serve the Babylon king seventy years; and it shall be when seventy years are accomplished that I will punish the Babylon king." This was uttered in 4 Jehoiakim, the very year in which the Captivity is supposed to begin.

(3) Jer. 29: 10—14. "Thus saith the Lord: When seventy years are accomplished for Babylon I will visit you and perform My good word toward you in causing you to return to this place . . . Ye shall call upon Me, and ye shall go and pray unto Me, and I will hearken unto you. . . . I will be found of you, saith the Lord, and I will turn your captivity." Uttered in 1 Zedekiah, eight years after 4 Jehoiakim, in which year the Captivity is already supposed to have begun.

§ 44. But the seventy years are found also elsewhere as follows:

(4) Zech. 1: 16. "In the eighth month in year two of Darius the word of the Lord came to Zechariah the prophet, son of Berechiah, son of Iddo, saying . . . Thus saith the Lord of hosts: Return unto Me, saith the Lord of

hosts, and I will return to you. . . . On day twenty-four of month eleven—the same is month Shebat—in year two of Darius the word of the Lord came unto Zechariah. . . . Then the angel of the Lord answered and said, 0 Lord of hosts, how long wilt Thou not have mercy on Jerusalem and on the cities of Judah against which Thou hast had indignation these seventy years? And the Lord answered: . . . I am jealous for Jerusalem and Zion with a great jealousy. . . . I am returned to Jerusalem with mercies; Mine house shall be built in it, saith the Lord of hosts, and a line shall be stretched forth upon Jerusalem."

(5) Zech. 7: 1—5. "It was in year four of Darius the king; the word of the Lord came to Zechariah on day four of the ninth month. . . . When ye fasted and mourned in the fifth and seventh [months], and this (too) seventy years, did ye at all fast unto Me?"

(6) In 2 Chron. 36: 11—23, Zedekiah "reigned eleven years in Jerusalem, and he did what was evil in sight of the Lord his God. . . . Moreover all the chiefs of the priests and the people trespassed very greatly after all the abominations of the nations, and they polluted the house of the Lord . . . they mocked God's messengers and despised His word and scoffed at His prophets, until the wrath of the Lord arose against His people till there was no remedy. Therefore He brought the king of the Chaldeans, who slew their young men with the sword in the house of their sanctuary, and had no compassion upon young man or virgin, old man or hoary headed, He gave all into his hand. And all the vessels of the house of God, great and small, and the treasures of the house of the Lord, and the treasures of the king and of his princes, all these he brought to Babylon. And they burned God's house, and brake down Jerusalem's wall, and burnt all its palaces with fire, and destroyed all its goodly vessels. And them that escaped the sword he carried away to Babylon; they were servants to him and his sons until the reign of the king of Persia; to fulfill the word of the Lord by Jeremiah's mouth, until the land had enjoyed its sabbaths; **as long as it lay desolate** it kept sabbath to fulfill seventy years, and in year one of Cyrus king of Persia, that the word of the Lord by [the] mouth of Jeremiah be accomplished, the Lord stirred up the spirit of Cyrus king of Persia, so that he made proclamation . . . . the Lord the God of heaven . . . . hath charged me to build Him a house in Jerusalem which is in Judah. Whoever is among you of all His people, the Lord his God be with him, and let him go up."

(7) After relating the events from Zedekiah's year 11 both 2 Kings 25: 21 and its parallel account in Jer. 52: 27 add, So Judah was carried away captive out of the land.

(8) Isa. 44:24 to 45: 4. "Thus saith the Lord . . . . that saith of Jerusalem, She shall be inhabited; and of the cities of Judah, They shall be built, and I will raise up its waste places; that saith to the deep, Be dry, and I will dry up the rivers; that saith of Cyrus, He is my shepherd, and shall perform all my pleasure, even saying to Jerusalem, She shall be built, and of the temple, Thy foundation shall be laid. Thus saith the Lord to His anointed, to Cyrus, whose right hand I have holden to subdue nations before him. . . . I will break in pieces the doors of brass, cut asunder the bars of iron . . . that thou know that it is I, the Lord, who call thee by thy name. . . . I have called thee by thy name, 1 have surnamed thee, though thou hast not known Me. . . . I will gird thee though thou hast not known Me."

§ 45. Passages (1), (2), (4) and (6) agree on a period of **desolation** of Judah. Passage (8) implies it, since it foretells a desolation of what in Isaiah's time, about a century before, was still in its glory.

Passages (1) to (6) all persist in the assertion that this period of desolation was to be seventy years.

Passages (2) and (3) assert that these seventy years of desolation, if not identical with, cover nearly the same period as, the bestowal of power on Babylon over Judah. When one ends, the other also ends, or is near its end.

Passage (3) promises restoration to Judah on repentance and prayer for deliverance.

Passage (8) names a century in advance the deliverer and restorer, Cyrus.

In Passage (4) the Lord calls unto repentance and prayer for the promised restoration.

In Passage (1) Daniel accordingly thus confesses and intercedes for Judah and Jerusalem, in the rest of the chapter.

Passages (6) and (7) begin this captivity of seventy years with the taking of Jerusalem and the king, and the destruction of the Temple in 11 Zedekiah.

Passage (4) marks 2 Darius as the last year of these 70.

Passage (6) marks 1 Cyrus as the year of the Restoration, and therefore as the year next to 2 Darius.

Finally: What Genesis 17, with all its minutiae, does for the identification of THE COVENANT Passage, (6), the last chapter of 2 Chronicles, does for the identification of the beginning of the Captivity. Hardly a line thereof but has a bell ringing therein, LO, THIS is the Captivity from which the Seventy years are to be counted; do not, oh do not mistake aught else for this! And dull indeed must be that betheorised ear that remains deaf to the pleading of that chapter.

§ 46. From these eight scriptures the following scheme is readily constructed:

About a century before his time Cyrus is named through Isaiah as the one who should restore Jerusalem and the Temple and the land of Judah from a condition of ruin, which at the time of the prophecy was wholly out of sight.

In 4 Jehoiakim, which is 1 Nebuchadnezzar, Jeremiah predicts a seventy years' captivity and desolation upon Jerusalem and Judah. At about the end of these seventy years Babylon, the desolator, would itself in turn be visited with wrath, and Judah restored if penitent and prayerful.

Jeremiah's prophecy duly begins to be fulfilled eighteen years later in 11 Zedekiah and 19 Nebuchadnezzar. Judah is led captive and Jerusalem laid desolate.

Daniel discovers in Jeremiah (in 1 Darius the Mede, year 69 of the Captivity), its exact length, and gives himself to repentance by confession, and prayer and intercession for the restoration of his people. The next year, in 2 Darius the Mede, the last of the Seventy, the angel of the Lord also inquires, Is not this the time for the end of Judah's affliction? The same year, the seventy years of Babylon's exaltation end, and it falls under Belshazzar to Darius the Mede, is related in detail in Daniel V.

With the fall of Babylon Judah's Captivity ends, and the next year, in 1 Cyrus he becomes the deliverer and restorer Jerusalem and Judah.

§ 47. With the year after 11 Zedekiah, or 3447 from Adam, (thus meeting the specifications required for the first year of the Seventy Captivity) are now to be compared the other captivities (if any) of Judah as candidates for the required Seventy years.

Four other captivities of Judah are recorded before 11 Zedekiah:

(1) Of Manasseh, only in 2 Chron. 33: 10—11. "And the Lord spake to Manasseh and the people, but they gave no heed. Wherefore the Lord brought upon them the captains of the host of the king of Assyria, who took Manasseh. in chains and bound him in fetters, and carried him to Babylon,"

(2) Of Jehoahaz, the first to reign of the three sons of Josiah who were kings. This captivity is related in both 2 Kings 23: 31—34 and 2 Chron. 36: 1—4. "Jehoahaz . . . reigned three months. . . . And Pharaoh Necho put him in bonds at Riblah in Hamath land that he might not reign in Jerusalem, and put the land to tribute. And Pharaoh Necho made Eliakim, son of Josiah, king in the room of Josiah his father, . . . but took Jehoahaz away and he came to Egypt and died there."

"Joahaz . . . reigned three months in Jerusalem. And the king of Egypt deposed him at Jerusalem, and fined the land a hundred talents of silver and a talent of gold. And the king of Egypt made Eliakim his brother king over Judah and Jerusalem, and changed his name to Jehoiakim. And Necho took Joahaz his brother and carried him to Egypt."

(3) Of Jehoiakim. Not recorded at all in 2 Kings; in 2 Chron. 36: 5—7, apparently so: but really recorded only in Dan. l: 1—3:

"Jehoiakim . . . reigned eleven years in Jerusalem. . . . Against him came up Nebuchadnezzar king of Babylon, and bound him in fetters to carry him to Babylon. Nebuchadnezzar also carried off the vessels of the house of the Lord to Babylon, and put them in his temple."

The parallel account in 2 Kings 23: 36; 24: 6 is : "Jehoiakim . . . reigned eleven years in Jerusalem. . . . In his days Nebuchadnezzar king of Babylon came up, and Jehoiakim became his servant three years. And the Lord sent against him bands of the Chaldeans and bands of the Syrians and bands of the Moabites and bands of Ammon's children, and sent them against Judah to destroy it . . . for the sins of Manasseh . . . So Jehoiakim slept with his fathers, and Jehoiachin reigned in his stead."

§ 48. Captivities (1) and (2) at once drop out of competition: since Jeremiah foretold the king of **Babylon** as the captor. Manasseh is indeed taken to Babylon, but it was then the capital of the king of **Assyria**.

Moreover, the captor was to be not any king of Babylon, but one specially named, Nebuchadnezzar. Jehoahaz is captive of the king of Egypt (see § 43, above, under 2, Jer. 25: 9—12). Moreover, the prophecy for the seventy years was given in 4 Jehoiakim. No Captivity therefore before that year can be the one needed.

And it is this year 4 Jehoiakim that for reasons which do not appear is the accepted year one of **the** Captivity, the (3) above.

From Kings we would not know that Jehoiakim was at all a captive. From Chronicles we learn that it was **intended** to take him to Babylon. But both Kings and Chronicles agree that he reigned his eleven years in **Jerusalem**. And as Nebuchadnezzar bound him several years before his death, and Jehoiakim died in Jerusalem, he apparently was not taken to Babylon at all, owing perhaps to a change of mind in Nebuchadnezzar. That he died in Jerusalem is clear from Jer. 22: 18—19: "Thus saith the Lord concerning Jehoiakim son of Josiah, king of Judah: They shall not lament for him [saying], Ah my brother, or Ah my sister. They shall not lament for him [saying] Ah lord, or Ah his glory. He shall be buried with the burial of an ass, drawn and cast forth beyond the gates of **Jerusalem**."

"In year three of the reign of Jehoiakim king of Judah came Nebuchadnezzar king of Babylon unto Jerusalem, and besieged it. And the Lord gave Jehoiakim king of Judah into his hand with part of the vessels of the house of God. . . . And the king spake unto Ashpenaz, master of his eunuchs, that he should bring: [certain] of Israel's children and of the seed royal and of the nobles, youths in whom was no blemish."

It is from this account of Daniel alone that we learn that there was a deportation in Jehoiakim's reign. And this deportation of certain youths for a specific purpose is mentioned only incidentally in order to account for Daniel's presence in Babylon. But for this incidental necessity, this captivity would not be known. Jeremiah and Kings are silent here, and Chronicles does not report here a **captivity**. Of the only persons actually reported as **taken** by Nebuchadnezzar, the report implies that the deportation of the king himself, though at first intended, was not carried out, presumably because of Jehoiakim's successful plea for himself that he had only been faithful to his hitherto Egyptian master. A plea of special force perhaps with a master who visited so savagely Zedekiah's rebellion upon him by first slaying his children in their father's sight, and then putting out his eyes: leaving the agonised father to carry this his last sight as the memory for the rest of his sightless days.

§ 49. This event thus fails of the two required specifications: there is no captivity of the KING, nor of Judah. The few of the royal seed with Daniel were apparently at first taken merely as hostages for Jehoiakim's fidelity to his new master. Neither is there the essential of DESOLATION of both Jerusalem and the land. The king is left in Jerusalem to live out his days there as king. Of the people, hardly any are deported. The only real deportation here was that of a part (and only a part) of the vessels of the house of God. None of these are qualifications for a captivity of king, princes and people, with the holy city and the entire land lying desolate for seventy successive years.

To reckon the 70 years from 4 (3 according to Daniel) Jehoiakim is thus out of question.

And thus the whole of Profane Chronology which is linked with 1 Cyrus succeeding the last of the 70 years—collapses. I Cyrus is some years further away than 70 from 4 Jehoiakim or 1 Nebuchadnezzar.

§ 50. There yet remains another candidate for the Captivity to be considered.

(4) Of Jehoiachin: Recorded in 2 Chron. 36: 9—10; 2 Kings 24 :8—17; Jer. 24: 1—10; and Ezek. 1: 2; 33: 21; 40: 1.

(a) 2 Chron. 36: 9—10. "Jehoiachin . . . reigned three months and ten days in Jerusalem, and he did what was evil in [the] eyes of the Lord. And at the year's turn king Nebuchadnezzar sent and brought him to Babylon with goodly vessels of the house of the Lord, and made Zedekiah his brother king over Judah and Jerusalem."

From this account alone we would only know that Jehoiachin was the only captive of this captivity, with some vessels from the Temple.

(b) Ezek. 1: 2; 33: 21; 40: 1. "As I was among the Captivity by the river Chebar . . . I saw visions of God. On [day] five of the month, which was the fifth year of the king Jehoiachin's captivity."

"And it was in year twelve, in the tenth [month], on the fifth of the month of our Captivity, that a fugitive from Jerusalem came to me saying, The City is smitten."

"In year twenty and five of our Captivity, in the beginning of the year, on [day] ten of the month, in year fourteen after the City was smitten, the self same day the hand of the Lord was upon me.

Here we learn that this Captivity was more extended than it appears from Chronicles. Ezekiel implies that he was led away captive with Jehoiachin: he calls it once, The Captivity of Jehoiachin the king; and twice, Our Captivity, his and those taken with him. Not of the nation, of Judah, for the City, Jerusalem with its Temple, was not "smitten" till eleven years after. Moreover, if the date of his own captivity is used by Ezekiel as an era from which he thus thrice directly, and other times indirectly, dates his prophecies, —he uses the destruction of Jerusalem eleven years later also for an era.

(c) 2 Kings 24: 8—17. "Jehoiachin was a son of eighteen years at his reigning, and he reigned in Jerusalem three months . . . . At that time servants of Nebuchadnezzar king of Babylon came up, and the city was besieged. And Nebuchadnezzar king of Babylon came upon the city, and his servants were besieging it. And Jehoiachin king of Judah went out to [the] Babylon king, and his mother and his servants and his princes and his officers. And [the] Babylon king took him in year eight of his reign. And he brought thence all the treasures of the house of the Lord and treasures the king's house, and cut in pieces all the vessels of gold which Solomon king of Israel had made in the temple of the Lord, as the Lord had said. And he took all Jerusalem captive, and all the princes, and all the mighty men of valour, captivity of ten thousand and all the craftsmen and the smiths; none remained save the poor of the land. And he took Jehoiachin captive to Babylon, and the king's mother and the king's wives and his officers, and the mighty men of the land he made to go captive from Jerusalem to Babylon. And all the men of might, seven thousand, and the craftsmen and the smiths a thousand all strong and apt for war Babylon's king brought them captive to Babylon. And Babylon's king made Mattaniah his uncle king in his stead, and changed his name to Zedekiah."

§ 51. This account greatly expands those of Ezekiel and Chronicles and makes it a captivity indeed. But (1) A king is still left reigning. (2) the City is not yet desolate. (3) The **land** itself is only incidentally mentioned here: the chief men and the poorest of the land. But of even these the "chief men" were presumably those living at court in Jerusalem.

Nevertheless this account makes this Captivity a rival, but the only rival candidate for the year from which the Seventy years are to be dated.

(d) Jer. 24: 1—10, "the Lord showed me: and lo, two baskets of figs set before the temple of the Lord, after that Nebuchadnezzar king of Babylon made a captive of Jeconiah, son of Jehoiakim, king of Judah; and Judah's princes and the craftsmen and the smiths from Jerusalem, and brought them to Babylon. The one basket had very good figs like the first ripe figs; and the other basket had very bad figs which could not be eaten for badness . . . And the word of the Lord came unto me saying: Thus saith the Lord, the God of Israel: Like these good figs so will I regard the captives of Judah for good whom I have sent out of this place into the land of the Chaldeans. For I will set mine eyes upon them for good, and will bring them again into this land . . . . And as the bad figs which cannot be eaten for badness, surely thus saith the Lord: So will I give up Zedekiah king of Judah and his princes and the residue of Jerusalem that remain in the land, and them that dwell in Egypt land. I will even give them to be tossed to and fro among all the kingdoms of the earth for evil, to be a reproach and a proverb, a taunt and a curse in all places whither I shall drive them. And I will send the sword, the famine and the pestilence among them till they be consumed from off the land that I gave unto them and their fathers."

Jeremiah is thus shown the exact relation between Jehoiakim's captivity and Zedekiah's. The one was not to be unto DESOLATION, but for good, as mere chastening. The other **was** to be unto desolation, and for evil as a punishment. It was indeed to be, as in 2 Chronicles, "without remedy."

Thus Jehoiakim's Captivity (already seven years after the received Captivity date), though the only rival candidate for the beginning of the Seventy years, falls also short of one of the required specifications, the— Desolation.

Canon VI thus **fixes** the Seventy years Captivity as beginning with the year following 11 Zedekiah, or in 3447 from Adam, and ending with 2 Darius the Mede, the year before 1 Cyrus, or with year 3516.

Thus just as the first Covenant with Abraham was only a covenant and not the covenant, and is accordingly left undated, so this first real captivity was a captivity and not the captivity, and is accordingly left without a desolation.

§ 52. To a similar disregard of this Canon VI is due another misplacement of two other important dates: the beginning and end of Daniel's seventy weeks of years.

In Dan. 9: 1, 16—19, "in year 1 of Darius son of Ahasuerus, of the seed of the Medes . . . in year one of his reign, Daniel prayed: O Lord, according to Thy righteousness let Thine anger and Thy fury, I pray Thee, be turned away from Thy city Jerusalem, Thy holy mount . . . Cause Thy face to shine upon Thy sanctuary that is desolate . . . Behold our desolations, and the city which is called by Thy name . . . O Lord hear, O Lord forgive, O Lord hearken and do; defer not, for Thine own sake, O my God, because Thy city and Thy people are called by Thy name. And while I was speaking and praying and confessing my sin and the sin of my people Israel, and presenting my supplication before the Lord my God, for the holy mount of my God, yea while I was speaking in prayer . . . the man Gabriel, being caused to fly swiftly, touched me.

§ 53. Daniel prays here not for the return of the captives to their land, for the restoration of the kingdom to Israel, but solely for the restoration of the **city**, and for the city only because of the sanctuary it was to contain. He was praying in 1 Darius. According to Zech. 1: 12 (see above § 43) 2 Darius was the last year of the seventy of Captivity and Desolation.[1] A year before its end Daniel thus prays, O Lord, DEFER NOT! He had already seen Babylon fallen to this same Darius; he had learned "from the book," from Jeremiah, that the time was seventy years; he knew also when these seventy years began. Immediately after his prayer he is told by Gabriel that though the Captivity and Desolations are drawing to an end, he is **at present** to look for nothing more than a temporal restoration to God's favour, that for the restoration of Israel to the kingdom under His own Anointed King centuries must yet intervene. "Seventy weeks [of years] are cut off for thy people and for the

---

[1] The commentators and chronologers, however, are unanimous in considering the Darius of Zechariah as Hystaspes, who reigned after Cyrus. Hystaspes is well known to Profane history, of Darius the Mede it knows nothing. The clearing up of the history of this particular period is beset with difficulties. The two most important authorities for this period are here apparently in hopeless discord. But that this Darius is a predecessor of Cyrus and not a successor is clear from the statement of the angel that the Seventy Years' Desolation are still on. All agree that at 1 Cyrus they were at an end. The chronologers and commentators, having already begun the confusion at 4 Jehoiakim as the beginning of the Captivity, could not but keep adding thereto as they went on. There still. however, remains this Biblical difficulty: The Bible allows apparently for Darius the Mede only two years, but Zechariah speaks in a later chapter of the fourth year of Darius, presumably the same king; but not necessarily, in view of the difficulty it creates. In any ease, it is clear that the 2 Darius of Zechariah preceded 1 Cyrus. even if 4 Darius should prove to have succeeded it. And a mere difficulty avails nothing against a certainty.

holy city . . . . Know therefore and discern that from the going forth of the word to restore and to build Jerusalem unto an anointed one, a prince, shall be seven sevens and sixty-two sevens; it shall be built again with street and moat in troublous times. And after the sixty and two weeks shall [the] Anointed one be cut off, and the people of the coming prince shall destroy the city and the sanctuary." (Dan. 9: 24—26).

§ 54. Daniel prays for the restoration of the city (for its sanctuary's sake), O Lord, **defer not**! He cries Delay not! because Babylon had already fallen, and was now in the hands of Darius the Mede. But according to the prophecies the fall of Babylon was to signal the end of the Captivity. So he prays, O Lord, defer not. The answer to this prayer was the proclamation shortly after by Cyrus for the restoration of the Temple; but with it Daniel is also told of a period 483 years with two specifications: (1) They are to begin with a decree to "restore and build Jerusalem": (2) they are to extend to "one Anointed, a Prince".

Daniel prays for the restoration of the **Holy** City. Cyrus is appointed some 150 years before his birth to say to **Jerusalem**, Be thou built; and to the Temple, Thy foundation shall be laid! Daniel's prayer is heard at once, and Gabriel is forthwith despatched to let him know that he is greatly beloved; that though Gabriel was delayed on his way three weeks, the delay was due not to aught in Daniel, but to resistance from the prince for Persia. His prayer for the **Holy City** he is thus assured is heard; and he is told that a decree is going forth to build the **City**. Cyrus does issue a proclamation to build the Temple, but in this proclamation no express mention is made of the CITY **but he issues no other proclamation**. This can mean only one thing: that in issuing the decree concerning the Temple, he was of necessity implying also the building of the City. For (1) the Temple could not be built without a settlement behind the builders for themselves and families; and the worshippers to come were sure to arrive by thousands. (2) In the mind of God and of all who have His mind, the City was built to contain His Temple, and not the Temple to adorn the City. Daniel accordingly kept praying for the city because of its sanctuary. The decree to build the Temple was thus from the very nature of the case a decree to build the City. The case must stand thus, or Daniel's prayer, in spite of Gabriel's assurance, was not answered; and Isaiah's prophecy to Cyrus was fulfilled only in part.

§ 55. This omission, however, by Cyrus to specially name the city has stumbled nearly all the chronologers, and they have for centuries been looking about for other decrees from which to date the 483 years. And as the decrees of Darius and of 7 and 20 Artaxerxes bring the 483 years beyond the birth of the Anointed of Daniel, these chronologers are compelled to say that the 483 years extend to (1) the baptism of the Lord, some thirty years after He was born; or (2) to the Cross, some three years later still; or even (3) to the destruction of Jerusalem, **seventy-three years** after the birth of the Messiah foretold to Daniel. But of the three decrees deemed by chronologers available for the purpose, the decree of Darius in Ezra 6: 1—12 does not mention the **restoration of the** CITY any more than the decree of Cyrus: since it is merely a restatement and confirmation thereof. Moreover, **it is not even dated**.

§ 56. The decree of 7 ARTAXERXES given in Ezra 7: 1—27 specifies three things: (1) Ezra and they like minded with him may return to Jerusalem. (2) Heavy offerings for the worship of the Lord in the Temple are to be taken to Jerusalem from the king. (3) Ezra is to institute civil government over "all the people beyond the River, such as know the laws of thy God." Ezra himself sums up this decree thus: "Blessed be the Lord, the God of our fathers. Who hath put such a thing in the king's heart, to beautify the house of the Lord which is in Jerusalem, and hath extended mercy unto me before the king." This decree thus deals only with the Temple and Government, but like the two preceding decrees says nothing about the **restoration of the City**. Moreover, Ezra's description of the king's desire to **beautify** the Temple implies that it was then already standing, but not yet in the glory befitting it. The utmost then that can be granted this event is that it might be admitted as a candidate for the end of the seventy years, as a rival to 1 Cyrus, but this not a single chronologer has so far proposed. And were even this claim to be considered, it could not be made good, because from the Bible it is impossible to say in what year from Adam Artaxerxes began to reign.

§ 57. The decree of 20 Artaxerxes thus remains the only rival of 1 Cyrus from which to begin the 483 years to the Messiah Prince. But Neh. (2: 1—9) had not asked for a **decree**, nor did Artaxerxes here make one. Nehemiah merely asked for letters to the governors of the parts through which he was to pass that they impede not his journey, and such letters the king gave him. Nehemiah in accordance with his request is thus granted, as a personal favorite of the king, his heart's desire to make Jerusalem a city with gates. A restored city it had already been for years, but the local enemies gave the Jews trouble, and Nehemiah was eager to restore Jerusalem not so much to a walled city, as to a city freed from these petty but serious annoyances. Nehemiah, as a private favour from the king obtained his heart's desire: but no decree, proclamation, or any other governmental act of record is mentioned here, as is specifically the case with three preceding events.

§ 58. But even if 20 Artaxerxes were otherwise an admissible rival to 1 Cyrus, it would lose its claim from the mere fact that 1 Artaxerxes being unassignable to any definite year by means of biblical data, the beginning of the 483 years remain uncertain.

1 Cyrus alone thus meeting the Bible specifications, it is the year from which the 483 to Messiah Prince must be dated. The Captivity (according to the same Canon VI which thus fixes its date) ending the year before 1 Cyrus, there is thus the only CONTINUOUS chronology to the Messiah according to the **Bible data**.

§ 59. The first specification by Gabriel "from the going forth of the commandment to build the City" is thus complied with by 1 Cyrus. The second specification is "to an anointed, a prince." This is by most taken to mean His baptism, when, they say, the Lord Jesus actually became the Messiah, the Christ. By others the entire 490 years (Gabriel says 483) of Daniel are brought down to the Cross, or even to the destruction of Jerusalem forty years later. In no case, however, are the 483 or 490 years here made out **exactly**. It is either "nearly," or "about," or the Jews were not particular as to their computing of the new moon, or the modern lunar tables do not always apply to Palestine moons two thousand years ago.

(a) The carrying down of the 483 or the 490 years "unto Messiah Prince" to the destruction of Jerusalem is on a par with calling Abraham's Call a Covenant, and with many like feats of even orthodox, yea evangelical modern Bible exegesis. No kingdom was set up at the destruction of the Holy City, but a Commonwealth was destroyed instead. The King, instead of then planting his feet on Mount Olivet, and sending then his law from Mount Zion, and about to rule the nations with a rod of iron, was then seated, at the right hand of the Father. If the Messiah then came at all, he came not unto salvation but unto destruction. And even this he did not accomplish in person, but sent "his armies to destroy their city." Only superficial exegesis can see in the destruction of Jerusalem the required arrival of Messiah Prince at the end of the 483 years.

(b) Neither is it at the Cross that the Lord became the Messiah, and certainly not then the Prince. Already some years before, the Lord accepted without rebuke the title Messiah at the hands of the disciples. In John 2: 1— 10 is related the Lord's first sign in turning water into wine. "This beginning of His signs did Jesus in Cana of Galilee, and manifested His glory; and His disciples believed on Him" (verse 11). The Glory can here be only of the Son of God, and the believing on Him can be only their acknowledging Him as such. In Chapter 1 before this "beginning of His signs," John Baptist announces the Lord publicly, Behold the Lamb of God which taketh away the sin of the world (verses 29, 36). In verse 34 he says, I have seen and have testified that this is the Son of God. In verse 41 Andrew tells Peter: "We have found the Messiah . . . . He brought him to Jesus. Jesus looked upon him and said: Simon, son of John, thou shalt be called Cephas," or Stone, presumably either because Peter had already acknowledged Him as Messiah, or the Lord then read this confession in his heart, which later before the Transfiguration was so distinctly and publicly made by Peter. Philip, in verses 45 confesses the Lord as the one "of whom Moses in the Law and the prophets did write Jesus of Nazareth." Nathanael confesses him in verse 49, Rabbei, thou art the Son of God, the king of Israel. The Lord here does not only approve the confession, He rewards it with the promise, Ye shall see angels ascending and descending upon the Son of Man. All this was some three years before the Cross. Nathanael actually confesses Him as the Messiah-**Prince**. To him He is the Son of God (Messiah) and King of Israel (Prince). Shortly after, the Lord, in John 4:26, tells the woman of Samaria that He Himself is the Christ she is talking about: "I that speak unto thee am He."

If only the Messiahship, therefore, is meant by an Anointed, a Prince, the 483 years cannot extend as far as the Cross, but only to at least three years before, say, to the descent of the Holy Spirit upon the Lord at His baptism, with the attestation from the Father, This is My Son the beloved in whom I am well pleased.

§ 60. But the phrase "an Anointed, Prince" contains not only the specification of anointing, Messiah in Hebrew, Christ in Greek, he must also be a Prince. Behold a king shall reign in righteousness, was the prophecy through Isaiah. Out of thee shall come forth a Governor, who shall rule My people Israel, was the prophecy for Messiah's birth-place. He was to be not only an Anointed one, only a prophet, or only a priest. He was to be Messiah-Prince, a King. This specification is accepted by most chronologers as met when a few days before the Cross the Lord Jesus entered Jerusalem and was greeted by a multitude as king, with the strong protest, however, from the rulers. This makes Gabriel's words to mean only, From the going forth of the commandment to an anointed KING, instead of, To an anointed, a prince. This forthwith splits up the fulfillment of the prophecy in two sections three years apart: The Lord becomes the Anointed at His baptism; He becomes the Prince within a few days of the Cross. This leaves the 483 years to oscillate between say 4029 and 4032 from Adam—a condition most unsatisfactory, specially so with a prophecy from God, and this too recorded in His own Book.

Every king beginning a dynasty had to be anointed. To make the 483 years end at **this** event as a sort of kingship of our Lord is not only to overlook the Messiahship of the Christ, it does also violence to the Hebrew. The position of the two words, Messiah, Prince, makes not for one office, an anointed prince (Prince Messiah would then be the order), but for an anointed one (whether prophet, or priest, or both) who is at the same time a Prince: a Messianic king, a Royal Messiah.

§ 61. Now the Lord Jesus (blessed be God) is indeed Prophet and Priest and King; and as all these offices require anointing, He was indeed the Anointed One, the Messiah (Hebrew), the Christ (Greek). But the assumption of each of these offices is separated from the others by an interval of time.

(1) In the days of His flesh, in the body prepared for Him of God, in likeness of sinful flesh, He was manifested to all only as the prophet foretold by Moses. He was also indeed King to all ready to own Him then as such. He was indeed the Saviour even of the world, to all those ready to own Him then as such. But the sin of the Jews (to whom alone He was sent in that body) consisted primarily in rejecting Him not as their king—they were willing enough to make Him their King if only on their terms,—but as the Prophet. Says Peter to the Jews in Acts 3: 22—26: "Moses indeed said, A prophet shall the Lord God raise up unto you from among your brethren like unto me; to Him shall ye hearken in all things whatever He shall speak unto you. And it shall be that every soul that shall not hearken to that Prophet shall be utterly destroyed from among the people. . . . Unto you first God having raised up His servant, sent Him to bless you in turning every one of you away from his iniquities." Having rejected Him as the teacher sent from God to teach them concerning Himself they debarred themselves from what was to be obtained from Him and through Him as priest and king: the law in His presence ever being, Except ye believe that I am He, ye shall die in your sins. As prophet He was sent to the Jews alone, and in a body in likeness of sinful flesh, and was visible to all and accessible to all.

(2) He became Priest, High Priest, when after being slain as the Lamb of God, and His blood is shed for the sins of the whole world, He enters the Holy of Holies, and there presents the blood shed. As priest He no longer has the body in likeness of sinful flesh. As priest He has the raised body, the

resurrection body. He dwells no longer on earth, though He may visit it; He now dwells in heaven, at the right hand of the Majesty on high; no longer, however, visible to all, but seen only of those to whom He is pleased to manifest Himself in His glory. As prophet His abode was on earth in a body visible to all.

As prophet and priest He is away from earth, His abode is in the heavens and He is not visible to all. The prophet is seen by saint and sinner alike, by every eye in fact, the priest is no longer seen by sinners. If seen at all it is only by the saint, and this too only on special occasions, and by the few.

(3) But as king He is again to be seen by all, by every eye, just as He could be seen as prophet. Only no longer in the body of the days of His prophethood, but in the body of priesthood. As prophet the Jews as a nation would not have Him. As the priest the world would not have Him. As the King both the Jews and the World **shall** have Him: the Jews willingly; but the World, whether willing or not,—"He **shall** rule the nations with a rod of iron." When the Son of Man shall come in His glory all the nations shall be gathered before Him. Then shall the King say unto them (Matt. 25: 31). And when in Rev. 19: 11—16 He whose name is there the Word of God comes forth to judge in righteousness, He hath also on His thigh the name King of kings.

So that the three offices of the Lord Jesus present a cycle of three stages in time:
Prophet,   seen by all
Priest,   seen by few.
King,   seen by all.
Each aspect of Messiah-Prince in its season.

§ 62. Hence though ever ready to be owned as King by all His subjects in every age, even the chosen sons of the kingdom, **He** assumes no kingship before the due season, and never **offers** Himself as king to Israel. Accordingly, in all the four Gospels, and throughout the three years' ministry, He is only four times recorded to have been greeted as king. And even of these four only two are sincere. At the Cross He was hailed king, but in mockery. When the multitude would **make** Him king, He departed from them. In John 12: 12—13 a politically unauthorized multitude precedes Him with the cry, Blessed the one who cometh in the Lord's name, the King of Israel. And the rulers, Israel's officialdom, promptly ask Him to rebuke the multitude. If He did not comply with their request, it was for reasons other than that of "presenting Himself as king to the nation." He told His disciples only shortly before that He was going up to Jerusalem not for the crown, but for the Cross. The only crown He knew to be before Him was the one of thorns. Nathanael had hailed Him as king of Israel, but he was a disciple, fresh in the glow of the discovery of the Messiah, and this too in the privacy of the interview. The Lord tolerated the enthusiasm of the multitude as He had tolerated Nathanael's. But while even Nathanael was most gently rebuked with the "Because I said unto thee I saw thee underneath the fig tree, believest thou? the multitude was not restrained: partly as a rebuke to the rulers ("if these held their peace, the very stones would cry out"); and partly that the prophecy be fulfilled, "Behold, thy King cometh unto thee meek and riding upon an ass" (Matt. 21: 4—5). The official accusation against the Lord that He had made Himself king is expressly declared by the inspired evangelists to have been—false. And Pilate himself, His judge herein, expressly declares, I find no fault in the man.

During His ministry and before the Cross the Lord was indeed already king, a king. and told Pilate so; only, Now My Kingdom is not hence, not of this world. He was already King by right, but not yet in fact. For this there were "times and season," He told the apostles in Acts 1: 7, and these "the Father hath set within His own authority." Too soon therefore it is to look on the Ministry or the Cross as the end of the 483 years to Messiah-Prince, if the open kingship is the one contemplated here. At the Ministry there is a Messiah, and one specification is met. There is no Prince, and the other specification is wanting.

§ 63. But if the Kingdom contemplated in prophecy is not as accepted of men on earth, but as bestowed of God in heaven, then the Ministry and the Cross are too late for it, just as for the other case they are too early. For there is in the book of God a definite point of time when in accordance with the mind of God the Lord Jesus is **declared** to be king. In Luke 1: 26—33 the angel Gabriel, who stands in the presence of God, was "sent from God" to say to Mary that the Lord Jesus "shall be great, and shall be called Son of the Most High (the Messiah) and the Lord God shall give Him **the throne of His father David, and He shall REIGN over the house of Jacob** unto the ages, and of His KINGDOM shall be no end." Son of God—Messiah; Shall reign—Prince. Gabriel, the same Gabriel who 483 years before told Daniel of a Messiah-Prince, now tells Mary that the one born of her shall be called Messiah, and shall be the Prince. Gabriel delivers his message to Daniel the year before the 483 years begin. He delivers his message to Mary the year before they end.

§ 64. Accordingly the New Testament begins with the genealogy which entitles Him to be the promised Prince, the one who has a right to the throne of His father David; and this beginning of the New Testament is duly followed by the narrative of the Magi. By a miracle specially for them they are divinely led to inquire for the One who to them is already King from His —**birth**. They ask, Where is the One born King of the Jews ? (Matt. 2: 2). In God's mind the Lord Jesus was already Messiah-Prince at His birth. And the only event meeting the two specifications of a Messiah and a Prince suitable for the end of the 483 years to that personage is the birth of the Lord Jesus, not the beginning of His ministry, which is thirty years later; nor the Cross, three years later still.

§ 65. At the time of His birth Messiah-Prince was expected: was expected by Simeon, expected by other faithful watchers who were looking for the consolation of Israel. He was not only expected, but sought out by the Magi from the East. All these knew the time when to expect Him, look for Him. But there was only one source from which the exact time could be learned: Gabriel's statement as to the 483 years. To all these watchers and searchers the 483 years expired at the **birth** of the Bethlehem Babe. Daniel had learned the end of the seventy years from a study of "the books," and acted accordingly. Simeon, Anna, the other watchers, and the Magi learned the end of the 483 years also by study of "the books," and acted accordingly. Daniel read his in Jeremiah, Simeon and his read theirs in Daniel.

§ 66. If the 483 years ended some thirty years later, the watcher at the time of the Child had no warrant for recognizing it as the Messiah-Prince. The statement has been seriously made that they knew the Messianic Babe because they knew that some thirty years later the 483 years were to expire. But apart from the fact that it is nowhere indicated that a king must be thirty at his manifestation, such "reasoning" would only equal the folly of propounding it.

But if either the Baptism or the Cross had met both of the required specifications, they have the fatal defect of not being—dated. The Lord was indeed thirty at the Ministry, and this lasted three years. But unless the Christ was born at the end of the 483 years, we know not from the Bible when the Lord was born; and thus we are ignorant as to when he was thirty or thirty-three. John Baptist's ministry is dated: 15 Tiberius. But (1) There is no certainty as to whether his sole reign is meant, or joint reign with Augustus. (2) The Bible does not enable us to say when Tiberius began to reign, whether jointly or alone. (3) Even if 15 Tiberius could be placed from the Bible data, this would only give the Ministry and the Cross approximately, it would not fix their exact date. All that is certain is that John was some six months older than the Lord, and that the Ministry began during 15 Tiberius or shortly after it. Unless, therefore, the end of the 483 years is at the birth of the Lord, we have no dates **from the Bible** for the birth of the Lord, nor for the Baptism, nor for the Cross—for not a single event **for which the prophecies of Daniel were given to be foreknown by God's people**.

§ 67. Thus just as the giving heed to Canon VI corrects the error of twenty-four years by the Received Chronology in the date of the Covenant, so it likewise restores the true dates of the seventy years of the Captivity (which is the only bridge from the Pre-Captivity to the Post-Captivity period) and Daniel's 483 years which succeed it: concerning which period the chronologers have widely departed from this Canon. Moreover, by leaving the Bible here for the Canon of Ptolemy, the accepted chronology has become a tangled skein where every twist or turn toward unravelling it entangles all the more.

§ 68. In accordance also with this Canon VI the face of the Bible Chronologer is set against the widely prevailing notion that certain numbers frequently recurring in the Bible may be taken at convenience as "round numbers."

Three numbers are frequently met with in Scripture: seven, twelve, and forty. While twelve is generally taken literally, seven at times and forty often are taken by not a few writers on the Bible as indefinite numbers.

§ 69. Now there may be cases where a number ending with zeros may not be exact, may be "round"; but it must be proved to be such either from the context, or from other data which compel the rejection of the literal sense. For mere assumption, supposition, opinion, the Bible leaves here no room whatever. Thus when David is said in 2 Sam, 5:4 to have reigned forty years, we are debarred by the next verse from unqualifiedly understanding it to be forty years **exactly**: "In Hebron he reigned over Judah seven years and six months; and in Jerusalem he reigned thirty and three years over all Israel and Judah." He may have thus reigned over forty years, the exact time over 33 years being given here as six months. In 1 Chron. 29: 27, however, "the time that he reigned over Israel was forty years." In the absence of the testimony from Kings some Chronologers would feel free here to understand the true number to be two-three years on either side of forty: say from thirty-seven to forty-three. The number 40 being frequently used in Scripture, it is forsooth a round number, or even an **indefinite** number. But the very next verse in Chronicles adds, Seven years reigned he in Hebron and thirty-three he reigned in Jerusalem. This division thus shows that the number 40 was meant to be definite and not round.

And yet even thus David only **may** have reigned over 40 years, but not necessarily. If he reigned in Jerusalem 32 years and a half, all the statements concerning his reign of 40 years are still true. It is certain that in Hebron he reigned seven years and a half. It is certain that for a consecutive Chronology his reign is given in all the three books, 2 Sam. 5: 4, 1 Kings (2: 11), and 1 Chron. 29: 27, as 40. The thirty-three years assigned to him in Jerusalem are therefore best taken not as full but current.

§ 70. In the New Testament there is no room for "round numbers." There numbers are carefully guarded from misunderstanding by the qualification "about" when needful. Thus in Luke 3: 23 "Jesus Himself, when He began was as if (about) thirty years [old]," thus distinctly warning that He was not exactly thirty.

"He had an only daughter **about** twelve" (Luke 8: 42). In Acts 13: 19 the Lord "gave their land for an inheritance for ABOUT 450 years," thus giving distinct warning that with the omission of the qualifying word the number would **not** be "round." Not even the 1,000 years of Rev. 20: 2 can be allowed to be "round," as long as after being introduced without the article (he bound him for **a** thousand years) in verse 2, the article is immediately after inserted thrice in verses 3, 5, and 7 ("until **the** thousand years be finished," etc.): meaning the definite fixed years exact.

In the Hebrew Old Testament, however, the writer is at present unaware that numbers are thus qualified at all. If numbers are there at all used as round they are easily shown to be such by the circumstances themselves stated in connection with them. Round numbers are therefore first to be proved as such, and not merely assumed as such. where their circumstances do not demand it.

§ 71. Thus the seven years of famine in Joseph's day are expressly divided into two and five (Gen. 45: 6). Jacob's 130 years, as he stands before Pharaoh (Gen. 47: 9), are protected as exact by "And Jacob lived in Egypt land seventeen years: and [the] days of Jacob's years of his life were seven years and forty and a hundred years" (Gen. 47: 28), 130 and 17 being 147. In the same way the 800 years of Adam after Seth's birth are protected against being taken as round by the statement that he was 130 at Seth's birth and 930 when he died (Gen. 5: 3—5). Jared's 800, Enoch's 300, Lamech's 777, Noah's 500 and 600, Enosh's 90, Kenafi's 70, Shem's 100, 500 and 600, and others like them, are carefully protected in the same chapter and in the eleventh. How the forty years of David are guarded by the division into seven and thirty-three, has already been shown above. The forty years of Israel in the wilderness are protected by the events named as occurring in the first, second, and fortieth years, as well as by Caleb's statement that he was forty in the second year of the Wilderness, and is eighty-five forty-five years later at the division of the Land (Josh. 14: 7—10). To assume, therefore, that where no such protection is in sight, numbers can be treated as "round" at the mere dictum of, say, the writers in Hastings' Bible Dictionary is sheer arbitrariness. From frequent unchallenged indulgence in this vice the Critics have come to look thereon as an indispensable part of their equipment. Accordingly Daniel's 70 weeks are to them a round number without ado: 77, though found only twice in the Bible, and 777 found only once, ditto.

It is as a guard against such presumptuous liberties with God's Book that Canon VI is specially effective.

§ 72. Canons I—VI thus prescribe the methods by which from the Bible data a consecutive Chronology can be readily constructed from Adam to the birth of the Christ. And with this once accomplished, the long-standing problem is solved, and the main task of Bible Chronology is, indeed accomplished.

The filling in, however, of the space's between these two dates presents now and then serious difficulties, bring to the apparent discrepancies between some of the Bible data: the periods from the Exodus to the Temple and from the Temple to the Captivity being herein peculiarly perplexing. So much so indeed that the adjustment of many of these dates has hitherto taxed to the utmost the ingenuity of all who have far honestly and competently dealt with them, but as yet without success. The solutions hitherto offered either depart from Bible data altogether, or they give them turns and interpretations which are impossible, and even fanciful. Still, even these might be tolerated, if only aught near unanimity were here at all within reach. But, except where the writers are only copies or mere echoes of one another, no two chronologers have yet to agree to agree as to a definite scheme of years for either of these two periods. Accordingly here is invoked Canon VII.

X. CANON VII.

The Reconciliation of what are apparently Discrepancies in the Bible Data must be along the Lines laid down in Canons I—VI; and any attempted Harmonization on other lines stands Self-Condemned.

§ 73. Thus Canon III requires that no textual error be charged upon the Bible unless demonstrated as such, and this moreover only by data from the Bible itself. Not merely suspected, nor even plausibly argued, but **demonstrated**. Canon IV requires that a clear Bible statement stand as against one not so clear: the light not to be obscured by the dark.

It has been shown above in §§ 11—16, 24, that the 480 years from Exodus to Temple are to be held to as demanded not only by one of these Canons, but by both. But it has also been seen in § 16 that the data of Judges, if taken as giving a **consecutive** Chronology, can be made to require for this period some 630 years (a length advocated by no one to the writer's knowledge). Likewise that the data in Acts, apparently based on Judges, can be made to require at least some 900 years. But with the length of 480 years taken as settled, not all the data of Judges can be taken as making up **together** a consecutive Chronology.

§ 74. Two ways of meeting this difficulty have been proposed by those who hold to the 480 years: (1) Some of the Judges were contemporary. This is indeed true of two of the judges: Samson and Eli were each contemporary in part with other judges. This is established from the data of the Bible itself: from Judges and 1 Samuel, as is shown in Part II. To this extent then this explanation satisfies Canon III. If, however, there were other contemporary judgeships (and these are needed in nearly all the schemes so far propounded), the Bible furnishes no data as to who were the contemporaries, and when; and all is left uncertain if not confusion, as is indeed to be expected when the Bible Canons are not complied with.

(2) A late school of writers, devout enough, and able enough withal, seriously propose the notion that though the period between Exodus and Temple does indeed cover some 580 years, yet the great God, in accordance with 1 Kings 6: 1, reckons only 480 years,—because for some ninety odd years of that period Israel, God's people, had been sinning, and in punishment was left for oppression by its enemies. And these periods of oppression are taken no account of in the **divine** chronology, however real they be in human chronology. Not one of the three writers, however, who

advance this "solution" gives the source of his information, which however is not in the Bible. This solution thus violating Canon VI at once absolves the writer from discussing it any further. Nevertheless it may be added that this "solution" creates more and greater difficulties than it removes. It contradicts other Bible **facts**: The forty years in the Wilderness were also years of sin; the seventy in Babylon were also years of punishment. The entire period of the rent-off kingdom of Israel was the result of the Lord's displeasure with His people. If the Oppressions in judges are "not divinely reckoned:" neither should these periods be. Moreover, there are three years in the history of the people of God, where this method of divine Chronology should he specially used, **if anywhere**. At the time of the Maccabees Israel was oppressed, as never before in its history and never after, by Antiochus Epiphanes for three years, with swine's flesh offered on the altar for the pollution of the Sanctuary. These three years are part of the 483 years from the Restoration to the Christ. If these three years are not "divinely reckoned," then this period's **real** length is not 483 years. but 486. But this correction every one of the three has failed to make in his Chronology.

The Lord God has set the sun and moon in the heavens for signs and **seasons**. He hath determined for the nations not only the bounds of their habitation, but also their **times** and **seasons**. Yet this "solution" makes the Creator of the time-pieces of the Universe (whose variation to even a second sets all the Observatories a-searching), play hide and seek with a whole century of time.

§ 76. With this method of Exegesis Noah may have lived more than 950 solar years, because the Lord God may not have been pleased to reckon that episode of the Vineyard. David may have reigned some years over the forty assigned him in the Bible; because God may have excluded therefrom those Absalom and Uriah days. And he of the, in 41 David, Absalom rebellion, may after all be right: only that the Higher Critic was for once here not quite so alert with his approaching omniscience as those three Orthodoxians.

These are the only two solutions so far offered, during the last few centuries in which Bible Chronology has at all been handled by earnest souls well equipped for their task. And neither of these two is found to serve the purpose. The true solution, however. is readily found, but only by the method of Canon VIII.

XI. CANON VIII.

In the Solution of Bible Difficulties that which Covers an entire Class of Cases stands as against those dealing with their individual Cases separately. The Simple Solution stands against the Complex.

§ 77. It having been shown that the data of Judges cannot be taken as successive (§ § 18—20), some must be eliminated as contemporaneous. There being, however, no ready clue in sight as to which are thus to be ignored in constructing a CONSECUTIVE Chronology for this period, the matter can be solved only by actual experimentation. It is then found that if the years of those oppressions (§ 20) which are succeeded in each case—and only these—by periods designated as "the land had rest" so many years, be included in these periods of rest, the chronology thus obtained meets all the requirements of the case. That is to say the Cushan Oppression of eight years is part of the forty Rest under Othniel. The Eglon Oppression of eighteen years is part of the eighty years Rest under Ehud. The Jabin Oppression of twenty years is part of the forty years Rest named at their end. And the seven years Midian Oppression are part of the forty Rest mentioned next. The omission of these fifty-three years thus justifies Jephthah's statement (§ 19) about those three hundred years; whereas if these fifty-three years be included, at least 352 years are required for the time covered by Jephthah's statement.

As no periods of Rest are mentioned after Abimelech's reign, though there were Oppressions by Ammon eighteen years and by the Philistines forty, these fifty-eight years are part of the consecutive Chronology for this period, and are accordingly not omitted like the other Oppressions.

§ 78. The sole purpose of the data for the length of these Oppressions is thus not to serve as links in the Chronology, but to designate their length. And Jephthah's 300 years are mentioned apparently for the express purpose of showing which of the Oppressions are to be omitted and which to be retained: a lighthouse amidst trackless billows, as if with a sign, **Here** is the channel, keep to this and avoid stranding. And the Chronology of this period has been hitherto admittedly hopelessly stranded.

That this is the true solution is readily seen in Part II under the years of that period. Seen, as a key is seen to be the right one when it first fits into the lock, and then opens it. But in Part III the Numerics for this period demonstrate it as well; showing that what is merely seen to be true cannot but be true.

§ 79. This result, however, at once rules out the interpretation hitherto given by all that "the land had rest forty [or eighty] years" means that the rest lasted 40 or 80 years: after the Oppression, by one set of chronologers; during the Oppression, by another set. The latter profess to find support in the fact that a period is sometimes spoken of as a whole when only a part is meant. Thus the period of the wandering of the sons of Israel in the Wilderness is frequently spoken of as one of 40 years: when in fact they were not condemned to be wanderers till the second year of the forty. And as that generation died in the fortieth year, they were wanderers less than thirty-nine. The wilderness period being in truth 40 years, the wandering also is spoken of as a period of 40. Other like examples occur. And indeed as a last resort this would have to be accepted here, but it is needless; since "the land had rest: 40 years"— the mere colon or dash would at once suggest the meaning as possible, and here necessary: "The land had rest [from oppression, ending a period of] 40 year." Forty years from the beginning of the history in the first case; 40 (or 80) from the last landmark, whatever it be. The "40 years" thus have nothing to do with the Rest. It is a mere chronological note which in modern writings would be relegated to a foot note, or to the margin, or at most be thrown into a parenthesis. But such ellipsis, as is frequent in Scripture (see the data at the beginning of the reigns in Kings and Chronicles), is not infrequent also in other ancient writings, and now and then modern writers who care for brevity of expression.

§ 80. By means of this same Canon VIII is settled the great difficulty of adjusting to one another the Chronology of the kings of Judah and Israel.

For the time from Solomon to the Captivity the dates are abundant, being determined moreover by three distinct lines: (1) The length of the reigns of the kings of Judah given in 1 and 2 Kings. (2) The length of the reigns of the Kings of Israel for much of the same period given also in 1 and 2 Kings. (3) The same data in 1 and 2 Chronicles. Kings and Chronicles, which are clearly independent sources (as is seen from the wide difference of method in dealing with the same events) entirely agree in their chronology, except in the case of the one (if indeed it is such) primitive copyist's error in Chronicles discussed below in Part II at Year 3109. But in checking the reigns of the kings of Judah with those of Israel it is soon seen that the **surface** meaning of the numbers cannot always be accepted as true; and the method must be sought out by which they are found scientifically to harmonise. Here too as in the case of the Chronology of the Judges actual experimentation is the only resource for extrication.

§ 81. In a series of dates of recurring events, presumed to be given for the purpose of accurate chronology, such as the length of reigns, the years given are either (1) full: or (2) current; or (3) partly full and partly current. With full years there is at once a scientific, consecutive Chronology. Add the years, and it is there. With the years reckoned as current (where a rein of, say, a year and a month is taken as of two years), there can still be a scientific Chronology if only due warning is given that the years are not full. Though even thus there is no certainty against confusion. But where the years are partly full and partly current, unless each case is specifically described as full or current, there is an end to a SCIENTIFIC Chronology.

§ 82. Thus at the division of Solomon's kingdom into those of Judah and Israel Rehoboam began his reign over Judah, and Jeroboam his reign over Israel, in the same year Year 1 of Rehoboam is thus also Year 1 of Jeroboam, and from here on the dates of the two sets of kings frequently interlock.

Rehoboam reigns seventeen years; his son Abijah reigns three years. He is succeeded by his son Asa, whose years 2 and 3 are specially dated in 1 Kings 15: 25, 28, 33, thus: "And Nadab, Jeroboam's son, reigned over Israel in Asa's year two" "And Baasha slew him in Asa's year three, . . . and reigned in his stead." "In Asa's year three . . . Baasha, Ahijah's son, reigned over all Israel." Rehoboam's 17, Abijah's 3, and Asa's 3. bring us thus to Year 23 of both Rehoboam and Jeroboam, according to the data far the kings of Judah. But according to the data for the kings of Israel, "the days which Jeroboam reigned were twenty and two years, and he slept with his fathers; and Nadab his son reigned in his stead" (1 Kings 14: 20). Nadab reigned two years, and was replaced by Baasha in 3 Asa, which was just seen to be 23 Jeroboam. But Jeroboam's 22, Nadab;s 2, and Baasha's 1, give not 23, but 25, two years more than for the same time covered by the data for Judah. Jeroboam and his son Nadab reigned therefore only 23 full years, and a rational explanation must be found for this 25. The explanation is simple enough. From the above quotations it is clear that Jeroboam reigned 72 full years, but Nadab reigned only one full year from 2 Asa to 3 Asa, though he reigned in two years. He is thus truly said to have reigned 2 (current) years.

Thus within the first quarter of a century from their common starting point the chronologies of Judah and Israel diverge already two years; and the very first case thus approached for close inspection meets us with a sign of Halt!

§ 83. The same result is obtained from a look at the next 25 years. In 1

Kings 15: 33 Baasha reigns 24 years, his Year 1 being Asa's 3. But "in year twenty and six of Asa . . . Elah, Baasha's son, reigned over Israel two years in Tirzah. . . . And Zimri came, and smote him and slew him in year twenty and seven of Asa" (1 Kings 16: 8, 10) From 3 Asa to 27 years. But Baasha's 24 and Elah's 2 give not 24, but 26 years. Thus at the end of another quarter of a century there is another divergence of two years between the Chronologies of Judah and Israel, the parallel columns being now thus four years out of line. And as these two sets of Israel's reigns are only examples of others, the lower down one goes, the greater the divergence grows, with apparently hopeless confusion at the end.

Into this confusion, however, order is at once brought if Baasha's 24 and Elah's 2 years are also. like Nadab's two years, taken not as full, but as current. Just as Nadab reigned only one full year but in two years.

The data for the kings of Israel thus do not prove available as a **standard** to which the data for Judah conform enough for a harmonised Chronology.

§ 84. Other is the case with the data for the kings of Judah in both Kings and Chronicles. For a continuous, consistent, scientific chronology they appear in no such unhealthy status. They do not indeed solve all the difficulties which are not few in this period, in spite of the abundance of data. But they lead into no tangle, no maze, no jungle, into which false systems of chronology soon conduct the student. In any case they leave fewer difficulties than on any other system known to the writer. It is demonstrated, moreover, at the proper place that, with the data for the kings of Judah once taken as the standard with which all others must comply, they alone establish the sought for harmony with the others.

§ 85. Accordingly, in this treatise, for the period from Solomon to Zedekiah, the lengths of the reigns of the kings of Judah are uniformly taken as of full years; and they are used as the standard wherewith to check the dates of the kings of Israel,—a method which, apart from the exigencies of the case itself, is already prescribed by Canon III: the clear being used for throwing light on the obscure: rather than letting the obscure darken the clear. And as the one simple expedient in Judges is found to cover all the perplexing data for its period, so this simple expedient for Kings is found to cover all the perplexities of its period. In Part 11 it is seen that this solution solves. In Part III Numerics demonstrate it.

By this the only method available for a **scientific** Chronology of this period four hundred and twenty-nine years are deduced for the time from 4 Solomon to 11 Zedekiah (from the Foundation of the Temple to its Destruction), which number 429 is neighbour to the 430 from the Covenant to the Law.

XII. CANON IX.

In Matters Biblical the Notions of "Unlikely, Improbable, Hard to Believe, Incredible, Inconceivable," and their like, are not to be Entertained so as to make the Bible Statements Void. Only what is demonstrably Irrational, or declared in the Bible itself to be Impossible, is to be allowed to Call in Question Bible Statements.

§ 86. With the Bible once accepted as God's book, its dictum stands that, With God **all** things are possible; and nothing is impossible save what the Bible here excepts. The question here is not what man **thinks** he can believe, but what **God says he** MUST believe. What God will or will not do, least of all what He is likely to do or not likely, is not for the worm of a man to opine about. He can know what God has **said** He does or does not, will or will not do. There is thus in things biblical no room for puny man to guess and to suppose, and surmise, or to opine, but solely in all humility to seek, and this moreover with due patience, to learn and understand what the great God **has** said in His Book.

According to this Canon, no statement however strange. however unlikely, however contrary even to experience, is to be dismissed without painstaking scrutiny, and above all not before **all** its possibilities have been exhausted.

§ 87. Thus in 2 Kings 15: 32 Jotham, son of Uzziah, reigns over Judah at twenty-five in Year 2 of Pekah of Israel, and he reigns **sixteen** years. In 2 Kings 16: 1 his son Ahaz begins to reign over Judah in 17 of Pekah. As 2 Pekah is 1 Jotham, 17 Pekah is 16 Jotham. And as in that year Ahaz. succeeded him, Jotham, according to these two passages, reigned 16 years.

In 2 Chron. 27:1, 8, it is twice said that Jotham was 25 at his reign, and reigned 16 years. Four times it is thus stated that this reign was 16 years.

But in 2 Kings 15: 30, before Jotham comes into view at all, it is stated: Hosea, Elah's son, conspired against Pekah, Remaliah's son, and slew him, and reigned in his stead in year **twenty** of Jotham, Uzziah's son.

As 16 Jotham was 17 Pekah, 20 Jotham was 21 Pekah. Pekah according to 2 Kings 15: 27, did reign 20 years. 1 Hosea is thus 20 Jotham and 21 Pekah. This statement thus harmonizes chronologically with the other four statements about Jotham's reign of 16 years.

But if Jotham reigned 16 years, and was succeeded **then** by Ahaz the mention of 20 Jotham is a difficulty, and Dr. Lightfoot speaks of it as Jotham reigning four years after he is—buried.

§ 88. This difficulty, with others like it, of which it is a good example, has stumbled not only those who like to find "contradictions" in the Bible, but even those who grieve at their possibility. To those who do not **love** the Book (and these are known by their fruits) Jotham's 20 years are "impossible," and to them is here demonstrably an "error." to those who do love the Book these 20 years **of Jotham**, with others like them, have only given occasion to offer remedies inferior only to the disease.

But first: The Bible does say that (1) Jotham reigned 16 years; and (2) he died. It does **not** say that he reigned 16 years, and **at their end he died**. In any other book such an inference is indeed allowable, though even here allowable only. But not in **God's** book, when ONLY TWO VERSES BEFORE 20 Jotham is named. Jotham may have lived some time after his sixteen years of reign (as did Napoleon, Charles V of Spain, and others). And this very mention of his year 20 may be intended to give notice of the fact that though his son Ahaz began to reign in what would be Year 17 of his father, Jotham was still alive in 4 Ahaz. There is nothing impossible in this, or even improbable.

The data in Kings and Chronicles are given primarily not much to tell how long each king lived, but how long he reigned: so as to provide a consecutive chronology for this period. Thus we know that David was 30 when he began to reign, and he reigned 40 years. He was thus presumably 70 when he died. The Bible does not expressly state the length of David's life. Of Solomon only the year of his accession is known, and that he reigned 40. When he was born, and how long he lived cannot be made out from the Bible.

But there is another possibility: Jotham's father was Uzziah, who was smitten with leprosy for presumption (Higher Critics, beware!) in acting as priest. Jotham thus ruled for his father some years, and the 20 years of Jotham may be reckoned from the time he thus became regent either with or for his father. And were this the true explanation, it would actually fix the year of Uzziah's transgression.

§ 89. This is the only case among the kings of Judah where the data given oblige us to accept an otherwise unrecorded joint reign of two kings, father and son: the case of David and Solomon being peculiar to the then situation, and lasting at the most a few weeks, at any rate less than a year. But with the kings of Israel the data more than once demand the acceptance of joint reigns. Though in no single case named as such, these alone harmonize the otherwise perplexing, yea insoluble difficulties presented by these data. Canon IX, however, covering as it does every such case, thus bring order here, just as the preceding Canons have brought unity and order into the data covered by them.

§ 90. A careful analysis of the data for Judah shows that one king was eleven when his son and successor was born: a fact truly hard to believe, and one indeed not to be accepted lightly. But this is hard to believe only for us. Oriental conditions of puberty and marriage differ widely from ours.

PART II.

PART II.
The Bible Data

§ 91. The data for a consecutive Chronology furnished by the Bible are of three classes:

(1) Those readily deducible from a plain statement of the text. Thus Genesis V furnishes clear data for the Chronology from the creation of Adam to 500 Noah, by giving the ages of each patriarch at the birth of his son. A further statement in Gen.7: 6 that the Flood was in 600 Noah thus brings the Chronology down to 1656 from Adam. The same is the case with the chronology from Arphaxad's birth "two years after the Flood," in 1658, to the death of Terah at the age of 205, in 2083 Adam, which is furnished in Genesis XI, by the ages of each patriarch at his son's birth.

(2) Those deducible only from more than one statement of the text: their combination being required in spite of the apparent plainness of each text separately.

§ 92. Thus in Gen. 5: 32 Noah is 500, and begets Shem, Ham, and Japhet. Standing alone this could be understood in only one way: the natural, plain sense being that at 500 Noah became father of triplets, of whom Shem was the oldest, and Japhet was the youngest. But in Gen. 11: 10 Shem is 100 when he begets Arphaxad two years after the Flood. The Flood was in 600 Noah. Two years after is 602 Noah. But if 100 Shem is 602 Noah, Shem was born not in 500 Noah, but in 502. And the statement in Gen. 5:32 that Noah was 500 and he begat Shem, Ham, and Japhet, must at once be modified in these three particulars: Shem was not one of triplets; he was not the oldest of the three, he was not born in 500 Noah, or in 1556 Adam. The statement, therefore in Gen. 5:32 can only mean that at 500 Noah was a father, and his sons were Shem, Ham, and Japhet; but who was born in 1556, whether Japhet and Ham as twins, or Japhet alone, or Ham alone, is left undetermined here. The only thing certain from Gen. 11: 10 is that Shem was not born then, but for reasons not given it was deemed best to name him first.

§ 93. Other Scriptures, however, make it plain, as shown below under Year 1556, that Japhet was the first born. This is also indicated in the genealogies of Noah's sons given in Gen.10: 1—32, and 1 Chron. 1: 4—27. Both these genealogies are indeed headed: Shem, Ham, and Japhet, presumably because "Blessed the God of **Shem**," as the one through whose line the Redeemer was to come. But when the genealogies are given in detail, the order is not Shem, Ham, and Japhet, but Japhet, Ham, Shem, according to priority of birth.

The case of Terah's three sons, given as Abraham, Nahor, and Haran, is parallel: Haran being the eldest, and Abraham the youngest of the three, as shown above for Abraham in Part I, § 28; and for Haran below under Year 1948.

(3) Those readily deducible from other dates, but requiring the utmost care in their adjustment, in spite of the apparent simplicity of the statements concerning them separately.

§ 94. Thus in Ex. 12: 40 "the sojourning of Israel's sons, who sojourned in Egypt, was four hundred and thirty years." Apparently this means that the sojourning began 430 years before the Exodus, which was within three months from the giving of the Law at Sinai. This then apparently began when Jacob at 130, Joseph being then 39, came with his sons to dwell in Egypt in Year Adam 2298. This might possibly be pushed back 22 years to 2276, when Joseph at 17 was brought a slave to Egypt. According to this statement then the 430 years of sojourning could not begin earlier than 2276. But, as shown in Part I, § § 26-27, the statement in Exodus 12: 40 can only be accepted in the light thrown thereon from Gal. 3: 17, which alone furnishes the true commentary on the term **sojourning**, as including Abraham and Isaac as "sons" of (spiritual) Israel; and the beginning of this "sojourn" is thus thrown back at least 169 years to 2107 from Adam.

In this particular case the light from Galatians upon Exodus is indeed clear. In other cases the matter is not so readily cleared up; and unless the utmost care is taken, inextricable confusion is the result.

§ 95. The number of individual years deducible from the Bible is 245, from Adam to the Cross, year 4032 Adam. After the Ascension in the same year, no dates are deducible from the Bible for the events mentioned therein.

These 245 years are indeed not the only ones that can be deduced from the Bible data—their number could indeed be manifolded. Thus if Adam lived 930 years, a complete Table of Bible dates could be made out, say, thus:

Year 1 from Creation,   Adam 1 year old.
Year 2 from Creation,   Adam 2 years old.
Year 3 from Creation,   Adam 3 years old.

And so on throughout his 930 years. Then in Seth's case the years could be continued after Adam's death thus:

Year 931 from Creation: Seth 801.
Year 932 from Creation: Seth 802.
Year 933 from Creation: Seth 803.

And so on throughout his 912 years. And as up to 2369 there is an unbroken chain of twenty-three generations from father to son, unto Joseph's death, there could thus be made out at once a list of 2369 individual consecutive years which could be truly deducible from the Bible data. But the individual events actually dated in the Bible during these 2369 years are only sixty-five. In the 930 years of Adam's life only two events are dated: the birth of his son Seth in his year 130, and his own death in 930. While, therefore, the Bible has thus at the very beginning as many as 2369 individual years deducible from its data, it offers no reason for entering, for purposes of Bible Chronology other than a small fraction thereof, the individual years it specifically names, or enables us to date.

§ 96. Similarly: The first of the seven years of Plenty under Joseph in Egypt was Year 2290. The last of the seven years of Famine was 2303. But of the fourteen years 2290—2303 only three are specially spoken of in the narrative: the last year of Plenty, and the first two of Famine. Accordingly, only these three of the fourteen are entitled to be entered among the dates making up Bible Chronology. And this applies to all the cases where a whole series of years is deducible from the dating of even one event: as the length of a life, or a reign, or a period, etc.

The only exceptions to this are the years of the births of individuals deducible from their other data, even though the birth itself is not dated. Thus the ages of most of the kings of Judah are given with the account of their reign. As the length of the reign is never omitted, the birth year is thus readily obtained. And through these individual years of their births are not specifically mentioned, they are uniformly entered among the 245 years. The same applies to other individuals. Thus when Caleb speaks of himself as 85 at the Division of the Land, the year of his birth is readily obtained; but though nowhere specifically spoken of, it is duly entered in the List. This principle applies throughout for every series of years connected with a **person**. The years beginning and ending such a series are always taken into the List, whether specially mentioned or not.

§ 97. On the other hand some dates, though they are apparently fixed in the Bible, can find no place in the List, because their fixture depends on other events which are not dated. Thus in Gen. 16: 3 "Sarai, Abram's wife, took Hagar . . . . after Abram had dwelt ten years in the land of Canaan, and gave her to Abram her husband to be his wife." This event is thus clearly dated: ten years after Abraham came to Canaan. Now Abraham started for Canaan at 75, on his father's death, in 2083; and Hagar's son Ishmael was born when his father Abraham was 86, eleven years later, in 2094. The ten years thus lie between 2083 and 2094, and could have begun only in 2083 or 2084, since they could run beyond the birth of Ishmael in 2094, and could not begin before 2083, when Abraham was as yet in Haran. But in which of the two years they began, whether in 2083 or in 2084, the Bible does not enable us to say. If Abraham came to Canaan the year his father died, in 2083, then the ten years ended in 2093. But if the burial of his father, the mourning for him, the settling of his affairs before the departure for a distant land, and the long journey itself to Canaan, took at least part of the next year, then Abraham came into Canaan in 2084, and the ten years run to 2094. If this is the year, it is already entered in the List of years as already deduced twofold: (1) from the statement that Abraham was 86 when Ishmael was born. (2) that Ishmael was 13 when circumcised with his father who was then 99. But if 2093 is the year, it would have to be added to the List, since no other event is dated for that year. As there is, however, no clear statement when the ten years began, 2093 rejected from the List, though Hagar's becoming Abraham's wife is clearly fixed to either 2093 or 2094.

§ 98. Joshua's death is thus likewise apparently dated in the Bible. He dies, like Joseph, at 110. But the date of Joseph's birth being obtained from the Bible data, his death is fixed at 2369. But Joshua's birth year is not obtainable, and the year of his death is left in suspense. He probably died in 2607, and thus was born in 2497, just one year before Caleb, his fellow spy, who was 85 at the division of the Land under Joshua. But there are no Bible data for fixing the year of Joshua's birth; and both the years of his birth and death are accordingly absent from the list of Bible years.

§ 99. Similarly: As Japhet was born in 1556, in 500 Noah, and Shem was born two years later in 1558, Ham was most likely born in 1557; in any case his birth is limited to years 1556, 1557, 1558. But the Bible gives no certainty as to which of these three he was born in, and 1557 is accordingly not given in the List.

The same is the case with the years of the births of the, sons of Jacob who were born before Joseph. As Jacob married Leah and Rachel after his first seven years of service, and Joseph was born at the end of the second seven, all the ten sons from Reuben to Zebulun were born only in the seven years 2253-2259; but the Bible data do not **fix** the date of a single birth of these ten to any definite year, and these years are accordingly not entered in the List.

Other examples the reader will readily find for himself.

In the following List, therefore, only those years are entered which are indisputably deduced from data furnished by the Bible: only those which are made **certain** thereby. The statements on which their fixture is based accompany therefore each year.

§ 100: For a consecutive Chronology the years given in the List must be reckoned as COMPLETE. Thus at the birth of Seth Adam is stated to be 130. That he was not then merely in his hundred and thirtieth year, but had completed them, is settled by the expression, And Adam lived 130 years, and begat Seth. This fixes Adam's age here as of 130 full years, and Seth's Year 1 is accordingly 131 Adam. But in most cases the expression is: He was a son of so many years. Thus in Gen. 21: 5 "Abraham was a son of a hundred years when Isaac his son was born to him." Here he was not necessarily full hundred years old: he may have lived up to then only 99 years, and be now only in his hundred**th**. Isaac's Year 1 thus **may** be 100 Abraham, and the time from father to son would thus be not 100 years, but 99. This is exactly what Beecher does in his Tables: he makes 1 Isaac to be 100 Abraham, and 1 Jacob to be 60 Isaac, thus shortening his own chronology by two years in these two instances alone from sheer oversight. It so happens that other Scripture makes it plain that Abraham was full hundred at Isaac's birth, but the expression **a son of** 100 years does not itself necessitate it. For the purpose of Bible Chronology, however, all such cases must be taken as full years: so that were even Isaac born in his fathers hundredth year that year would chronologically have to be reckoned to Abraham, and 1 Isaac would be the equivalent only of 101 Abraham. Without this method (which applies to all data forming a series), there can be no certain consecutive, and hardly any scientific chronology.

§ 101. The translation of the Scriptures which accompanies the years in the List is directly from the original, for the reasons given in Part I, Chapters VIII. and IX. Words of the translation not in the original are in brackets, (chiefly the article), or in bold type. At the end of the Scripture quotations given for each year the calculation is given by which the number is arrived at, except in the case of the second two consecutive years. Thus it is omitted for 1657, since 1656 precedes it in the List.

YEARS DEDUCIBLE FROM THE DATA OF THE BIBLE.

Seth born   Adam 130   **Year 130.**

And Adam lived thirty and a hundred years and he begat . . . . Seth.   Gen. 5: 3.

Enosh born   Seth 105   **Year 235.**

And Seth lived five years and a hundred years, and he begat Enosh.   Gen. 5: 6.

Seth was born in 130; and 105 are 235.

Kenan born   Enosh 90   **Year 325.**

And Enosh lived ninety years, and he begat Kenan. Gen. 5: 9.

Enosh was born in 235; and 90 are 325

Mahalaleel born   Kenan 70   **Year 395.**

And Kenan lived seventy years, and he begat Mahalaleel.

Gen. 5: 12.

Kenan was born in 325; and 70 are 395.

Jared born   Mahalaleel 65   **Year 460.**

And Mahalaleel lived five years and sixty years, and he begat Jared.   Gen. 5: 15.

Mahalaleel was born in 395; and 65 are 460

Enoch born   Jared 162   **Year 622.**

And Jared lived two and sixty years, and he begat Enoch.

Jared was born in 460; and 162 are 622.   Gen. 5: 18.

Methuselah born　　　　　Enoch 65　　　　　　　　**Year 687.**

And Enoch lived five and sixty years and a hundred years, and he begat Methuselah.　　　　　　　　　　Gen. 5: 21.

Enoch was born in 622; and 65 are 687.

Lamech born　　　　　Methuselah 187　　　　　　**Year 874.**

And Methuselah lived seven and eighty years and a hundred years, and he begat Lamech.　　　　　　　　Gen. 5: 25.

Methuselah was born 687; and 187 are 874.

Adam dies, age 930　　　　　　　　　　　　　　**Year 930.**

And all [the] days which Adam lived were nine hundred years and thirty years.　　　　　　　　　　　　　Gen. 5: 5.

Enoch Translated, aged 365　　　　　　　　　　**Year 987.**

And all [the] days of Enoch were five and sixty years and three hundred years. And Enoch walked with God, and he was not; for God took him. Gen. 5: 23.

Enoch was born in 622; and 365 are 987.

Seth dies, age 912.　　　　　　　　　　　　　　**Year 1042.**

And all the days of Seth were twelve years and nine hundred years.　　　　　　　　　　　　　　　　　Gen. 5: 8.

Seth was born in 130; and 912 are 1042.

Noah born.　　　　　Lamech 182　　　　　　　　**Year 1056.**

And Lamech lived two and eighty years and a hundred years and begat Noah.　　　　　　　　　　　　　Gen. 5: 28.

Lamech was born in 874; and 182 are 1056.

Enosh dies, aged 905.   **Year 1140.**

And all [the] days of Enosh were five years and nine hundred years.   Gen. 5: 11.

Enosh was born in 235; and 905 are 1140.

Kenan dies, age 910   **Year 1235.**

And all [the] days of Kenan were ten years and nine hundred years.   Gen. 5: 14.

Kenan was born in 325; and 910 are 1235.

Mahalaleel dies, age 895   **Year 1290.**

And all [the] days of Mahalaleel were five and ninety years and eight hundred years.   Gen. 5: 17.

Mahalaleel was born in 395; and 895 are 1290.

Jared dies, age 962   **Year 1290.**

And all [the] days of Jared were two and sixty years and nine hundred years.   Gen. 5: 17.

Jared was born in 460; and 962 are 1442.

Flood decreed.   **Year 1536.**

And the Lord said, My Spirit shall not strive with man for ever, for that he also is flesh; and his days shall be a hundred and twenty years. Gen. 6: 3.

The Flood took place in Year 1656 (which see): this less 120 is 1536. This passage is understood thus only by some: by others it is not taken as a prophecy, in which case the year 1536 drops out as a Bible date. The Bible itself throws no light on the true interpretation here. Numerics, however, as is demonstrated in Part III, show that this year is dated in the Bible, and this passage is therefore a prophecy of warning for 120 years of a Flood.

Japhet born.   Noah 500   **Year 1556.**

And Noah was a son of five hundred years, and he begat Shem, Ham, and Japhet. Gen. 5: 32.

Noah was born in 1056; and 500 are 1556.

See above § § 92—93. That Shem was not born till 1558 is seen under that year. In Gen. 9: 24 "Noah awoke from his wine, and knew what his son had done to him." Ham is here meant, and referred to as the **little**, the idiom for **younger**, when as here others are also spoken of. Japhet and Shem are named in the preceding verse. In Gen. 10: 21 Japhet is mentioned thus: "And unto Shem. . . . brother of Japhet the great"—idiom for **elder**. Japhet being thus the elder brother of Shem, and Ham being the younger, it is Japhet that was born in 1556; though the possibility is not excluded, as far as this text is concerned, that Japhet and Ham were twins. But though the birth of Ham is not dated, Numerics favour 1557 as the year of Ham's birth: the dates of the three brothers thus being 1556, 1557, 1558.

Moreover, in other cases of twins as those of Esau and Jacob, Pharez and Zerah, it is stated that twins they are. Here it is not so stated. The probability therefore that Ham was a twin is thus greatly reduced. But as Ham's birth is not spoken of in the Bible, except when mentioned with his brothers, and is not deducible from other texts, the year 1557 has no place among the **Bible** years.

See below for the case of Abram, Nahor and Haran, parallel to that of Shem, Ham, and Japhet, under Year 1948.

Shem born. **Year 1558.**

Shem was a son of a hundred years, and he begat Arphaxad two years after the Flood. Gen. 11:10.

The Flood was in 1656, which see. Shem is thus 100 two years later, in 1658; less 100 are 1558.

Lamech dies, age 777 **Year 1651.**

And all [the] days of Lamech were seven and seventy years and seven hundred years. Gen. 5: 31.

Lamech was born in 874; and 777 are 1651.

Methuselah dies, age 969.   **The Flood, Year 1656.**

And all [the] days of Methuselah were nine and sixty years and nine hundred years.

And Noah was a son of six hundred years, and the Flood was upon the earth.   Gen. 5: 27; 7: 6.

Methuselah was born in 687; and 969 are 1656. Noah was born in 1056; and 600 are also 1656.

Noah 601.   Flood ends.   **Year 1657.**

And it was in year one and six hundred, in the first [month], in (day) one of the month—the waters dried off from over the earth.
Gen. 8: 13.

Arphaxad born.   Shem 100.   **Year 1658.**

Shem . . . begat Arphaxad two years after the flood.

                                                                 Gen 11: 10.

Shelah born.   Arphaxad 35.   **Year 1693.**

And Arphaxad lived five and thirty years, and he begat
Shelah.   Gen. 11: 12.

Arphaxad was born in 1658; and 35 are 1693.

Eber born.   Shelah 30.   **Year 1723.**

And Shelah lived thirty years, and he begat Eber. Gen. 11:14.

Shelah was born in 1693; and 30 are 1723.

Peleg born.   Eber 34.   **Year 1757.**

And Eber lived four and thirty years, and he begat Peleg.

                                                                 Gen. 11: 16.

Eber was born in 1723; and 34 are 1757.

Reu born.   Peleg 30.   **Year 1787.**

And Peleg lived thirty years, and he begat Reu.   Gen. 11: 18.

Peleg was born in 1757; and 30 are 1787.

Serug born.   Reu 32.   **Year 1819.**

And Reu lived two and thirty years, and he begat Serug.

Gen. 11: 20.

Reu was born in 1787; and 32 are 1819.

Nahor born.   Serug 30.   **Year 1849.**

And Serug lived thirty years, and he begat Nahor.

Gen. 11: 22.

Serug was born in 1819; and 30 are 1849.

Terah born.   Nahor 29.   **Year 1878.**

And Nahor lived nine and twenty years, and he begat Terah.

Gen. 11: 24.

Nahor was born in 1849; and 29 are 1878.

Haran born.   Terah 70.   **Year 1948.**

And Terah lived seventy years, and he begat Abram, Nahor, and Haran.

Gen. 11: 26.

Terah was born in 1878; and 70 are 1948.

That it was not Abraham that was born when Terah was 70 was shown in Part I, § 28. Compare also § 93 and Year 1556. All that is meant in Gen. 11: 26 is that Terah was 70 when he became a father, and his sons were Abram, Nahor and Haran: of whom Abram is named first not because the oldest, but because the Redeemer was to be through his line: the case of Abraham being parallel with that of Shem. Scripture, however, does not make it certain that it was Haran rather than Nahor that was born in 70 Terah; nor that the two older brothers were not twins, unless light be thrown hereon by Numerics. These questions do not affect the **Chronology**, the only question being as to what person shall be named as born in 1948: Haran or Nahor, and this is not a strictly Bible Chronology question.

That Haran, however, was the older rather than Nahor is suggested already by the order of Shem, Ham, and Japhet: where the oldest is put last, the three being given in the reverse order of their age.

Peleg dies, age 239.   **Year 1996.**

    And Peleg lived after he begat Reu nine years and two hundred years.   Gen. 11: 19.

    Reu was born in 1787; and 209 are 1996.

Nahor dies, age 148.   **Year 1997.**

    And Nahor lived after he begat Terah nineteen years and a hundred years.   Gen. 11: 25.

    Terah was born in 1878; and 119 are 1997.

Noah dies, age 950.   **Year 2006.**

    All the days of Noah were nine hundred years and fifty years.

                                                                                             Gen. 9: 29.

    Noah was born in 1056; and 950 are 2006.

Abraham born.   **Year 2008.**

    See under 1948 that it was not Abraham that was born at 70 Terah; and see part 1, § 28, that Abraham was born at 130 Terah.

    Terah was born in 1878; and 130 are 2008.

Sarah born.   **Year 2017.**

    And Abraham fell on his face and laughed; and said in his heart, Shall one be born to a son of a hundred years, and shall Sarah, daughter of ninety years bear?   Gen. 17: 17.

    Abraham was born in 2008. At his 99 Sarah is 90. She was thus born nine years after Abraham. 2008 and 9 are 2017.

    All chronologers make Sarah ten years younger than her husband, which makes her birth in 2018, one year later; but this misapprehends Gen. 17: 17. When Abraham thus laughs at the Lord's promise of a son from **Sarah**, who is THEN 90, Abraham himself is not 100, but 99 according to verse 1: And Abram was a son of ninety years and nine years; and the Lord appeared unto

Abram and said to him, etc. Sarah is thus 90 when he is 99. When Abram speaks of 100 when he is 99, he is thinking of the time next year when the child shall be actually **born**. Shall one be born to [me when I am] a son of a hundred years, and shall Sarah [now] a daughter of ninety years bear? Sarah is thus nine years Abraham's junior, not 10. Numerics, moreover, demonstrate conclusively that Sarah's birth year is 2017, not 2018. And as Sarah died 127 years later, the year of her death is also affected thereby, and moves down one year also.

Reu dies, age 239.   **Year 2026.**

And Reu lived after he begat Serug seven years and two hundred years.   Gen. 11: 21.

Serug was born in 1819; and 207 are 2026.

Serug dies, age 230.   **Year 2049.**

And Serug lived after he begat Nahor two hundred years.   Gen. 11: 23.

Nahor was born in 1849; and 200 are 2049.

Terah dies, age 205.   **Year 2083.**

And Terah's days were five years and two hundred years.   Gen. 11: 32.

Terah was born in 1878; and 205 are 2083.

Ishmael born.   Abraham 86.   **Year 2094.**

And Abraham was a son of eighty years and six years when Hagar bare Ishmael to Abram.   Gen. 16: 16.

Abraham was born in 2008; and 86 are 2094.

Arphaxad dies, age 438.   **Year 2096.**

And Arphaxad lived after he begat Shelah three years and four hundred years.   Gen. 11:13.

Shelah was born in 1693; and 403 are 2096.

Abraham 99.   The Covenant.   **Year 2107.**

And Abram was a son of ninety years and nine years.

Gen. 17: 1.

See part I, § § 34—40, for the other Scriptures for this year, and the proof that this is the year of the Covenant.

Abraham was born in 2008; and 99 are 2107.

Isaac born.   Abram 100.   **Year 2108.**

And Abraham was a son of a hundred years when his son Isaac was born to him.

Gen. 21: 5.

Abraham was born in 2008; and 100 is 2108.

Shelah dies, age 403[2].   **Year 2126.**

And Shelah lived after he begat Eber three years and four hundred years.

Gen. 11: 15.

Eber was born in 1723; and 403 are 2126.

Sarah dies, age 127.   **Year 2144.**

And Sarah's life was a hundred years and twenty years and seven years.

Gen. 23: 1.

Sarah was born in 2017; and 127 is 2144.

Isaac 40. Marries Rebecca.   **Year 2148.**

And Isaac was a son of forty years when he took Rebecca . . . for **his** wife.

Gen. 25: 20.

Isaac was born in 2108; and 40 are 2148.

Shem dies, age 600.   **Year 2158.**

And Shem lived after he begat Arphaxad five hundred years.

---

2   The 1950 reprint erroneously has "433" here, which has been corrected in this 2014 edition.

Gen. 11: 11.

Arphaxad was born in 1658; and 500 are 2158.

Jacob and Esau born.　　　　Isaac 60.　　　　**Year 2168.**

And Isaac was a son of sixty years when she (Rebecca) bare them (Esau and Jacob).　　　　Gen. 25: 26.

Isaac was born in 2108; and 60 are 2168.

Abraham dies, age 175.　　　　**Year 2183.**

And these are the days of the years of Abraham's life which he lived: a hundred years, seventy years and five years.

Gen. 25: 7.

Abraham was born in 2008; and 175 are 2183.

Eber dies, age 464.　　　　**Year 2187.**

And Eber lived after he begat Peleg thirty years and four hundred years.　　　　Gen. 11:17.

Peleg was born in 1757; and 430 are 2187.

Esau 40. Marries Judith.　　　　**Year 2208.**

And Esau was a son of forty years, and he took Judith for a wife.　　　　Gen. 26:34.

Esau was born in 2168; and 40 are 2208.

Ishmael dies; age 137.　　　　**Year 2231.**

And these are the years of Ishmael's life: a hundred years and thirty years and seven years.　　　　Gen. 25:17.

Ishmael was born in 2094; and 137 are 2231.

Jacob begins to serve Laban at 77.　　　　**Year 2245.**

Jacob was born in 2168 and 77 are 2245.

In Gen. 41: 46 "Joseph was a son of thirty years when he stood before Pharaoh." foretelling the seven years of plenty and the seven years of famine to follow. The years of plenty begin at once in the next verse: "And the land brought forth in seven plenteous years by handfuls." "And the seven years of plenty came to an end . . . And the seven years of famine began to come" (Gen. 41: 53—54). Joseph is thus now 37. Jacob arrives in Egypt and is presented to Pharaoh in the year when Joseph sends word to him to come: "these two years hath the famine been in the land, and five years are yet." "There are yet five years of famine" (Gen. 45: 6, 11). Joseph is thus now 39. But in Gen. 47: 8—9 "Pharaoh said to Jacob, How many are the days of your life's years? And Jacob said to Pharaoh, The days of the years of my pilgrimage are thirty and a hundred years." Jacob is thus 130 when Joseph is 39; he was thus 91 when Joseph was born. In Gen. 31: 41 Jacob says to Laban: These twenty years have I been in thy house. I served thee fourteen years for thy two daughters, and six years for thy flock.

In Gen. 30: 25 "it came to pass when Rachel had borne Joseph that Jacob said to Laban: Send me away that I may go unto mine own place and my country." The rest of the chapter tells of the arrangement between Jacob and Laban that Jacob now works for his flocks as he had served the preceding fourteen for his wives. Joseph was thus born at the end of Jacob's 14 years with Laban. If 91 at the birth of Joseph, at the end of 14 years' service, Jacob is 77 when he begins to serve.

Jacob 84. Marries Leah and Rachel.   Year 2252.

And Jacob served for Rachel 7 years.   Gen. 29: 20.

Jacob's service began in 2245; and 7 are 2252.

Joseph born.   Jacob 91.   Year 2259.

See under 2245 that Joseph was born when Jacob was 91.

Jacob was born in 2168; and 91 are 2259.

Jacob 97. Leaves Laban.   Year 2265.

These twenty years have I been in thine house—Jacob to

Laban.   Gen. 31: 41.

Jacob came to Laban 2245; and 20 are 2265.

Joseph 17. Sold by his brethren.   **Year 2276.**

Joseph, a son of seventeen years, was shepherding with his brethren, ... and they sold Joseph.   Gen. 37: 2, 28.

Joseph was born in 2259; and 28 are 2287.

Joseph 28. In prison.   **Year 2287.**

And it came to pass at **the** end of two years' days that Pharaoh dreamed.   Gen. 41: 1.

Joseph was born in 2259; and 28 are 2287.

This dream was the cause of Joseph's standing before Pharaoh, when he was 30, as seen under 2289. He was in prison therefore at 28.

Isaac dies, age 180.   **Year 2288.**

And the days of Isaac were a hundred years and eighty years.

                                    Gen. 35: 28.

Isaac was born in 2108; and 180 are 2288.

Joseph 30, Stands before Pharaoh.   **Year 2289.**

And Joseph was a son of thirty years when he stood before Pharaoh.   Gen. 41: 46.

Joseph was born in 2259; and 30 are 2289.

7 Years of Plenty end.   **Year 2296.**

And the seven years of plenty ended.   Gen. 41: 53.

Joseph foretold them in 2289; and 7 are 2296.

Year 1 of Famine.   **Year 2297.**

And the seven years of famine began to come.   Gen. 41: 54.

Year 2 of Famine.   **Year 2298.**

These two years hath the famine been.   Gen 45: 6.

See also under 2245.

Jacob dies, age 147.   **Year 2315.**

And the days of the years of Jacob's life were seven years and forty and a hundred years.   Gen. 47: 28.

Jacob was born in 2168; and 147 are 2315.

Joseph dies, age 110.   **Year 2369.**

And Joseph died, a son of a hundred and ten years.

Gen. 50: 26.

Joseph was born in 2259; and 110 are 2369.

Aaron born.   **Year 2454.**

And Moses was a son of eighty years, and Aaron a son of three and eighty years when they spake to Pharaoh.

Ex. 7: 7.

This was shortly before the Exodus in 2537 (which see): less 83 is 2454.

Moses born.   **Year 2457.**

See year 2454. Moses was born three years after Aaron, who was born 2454; and 3 are 2457.

Moses 40.   **Year 2497.**

And Moses . . . when a forty years' time was fulfilled unto him, it came into his heart to visit his brethren.   Act. 7: 23.

Moses was born in 2457; and 40 are 2497.

Caleb born.   **Year 2498.**

Caleb was 40 in 2538; less forty are 2498.

Caleb and Joshua were of the twelve sent to spy out the land. The evil report brought back by the other ten caused the Congregation to murmur: for which they were condemned to be wanderers 40 years in the wilderness. "Your children shall be wanderers forty years" (Numb. 14: 33). But this sentence was passed upon them after "it came to pass in the second year, in

day twenty of the month" of Numb. 10: 11; and "the Lord spake unto Moses in the Sinai wilderness in the second year from their leaving Egypt land" (Numb. 9: 1). The Exodus was in 2537, which see. This is, therefore, in 2538 when Caleb is sent to spy out the land. In Josh. 14: 7 Caleb says, A son of forty years I was when Moses, the servant of the Lord, sent me from Kadesh Barnea to spy out the land. He was thus sent out at the age of forty in 2538.

The Exodus. The Law.   Year 2537.

And Moses was a son of eighty years, and Aaron a son of three and eighty years, when they spake to Pharaoh.   Ex. 7: 7.

Moses was born in 2457; and 80 are 2537.

Aaron was born in 2454; and 83 are 2537.

Moses and Aaron stood before Pharaoh not earlier than the year of the Exodus, since they died in Year 40 from the Exodus: the one 120 years old, and the other 123, as is seen under Year 2576. The Exodus is: "And it came to pass at the end of thirty years and four hundred years, and it came to pass the self-same day that the hosts of the Lord all went out from Egypt land" (Ex. 12: 41). As the Law was given only a few weeks after this Exodus ("in the third month after Israel's sons were gone forth out of Egypt land, on this day they came into the Sinai wilderness," Ex. 19: 1), these four hundred and thirty years are the same as in Gal. 3: 16—17 from the Law back to the Covenant with Abraham. "Now to Abraham were the promises spoken . . . . A covenant confirmed beforehand by God the Law which came four hundred and thirty years after doth not disannul." These 430 years date, therefore, from the Covenant in 2107; and the Law was thus given in 2537.

Exodus Year 2.   Caleb 40.   Year 2538.

And the Lord spake to Moses in the Sinai Wilderness in the second year from their leaving Egypt land.   Numb. 9: 1.

Exodus Year 40.   Moses dies, age 120; and   Year 2576.
                          Aaron dies, age 123.

And it came to pass in year forty, in month eleven, in day one of the month, Moses spake unto Israel's sons.   Deut. 1: 3.

And Aaron the priest went up Mount Hor, . . . and died there in year forty of the departure of Israel's sons from Egypt, in the fifth month, on **day** one of the month. And Aaron was a son of three and twenty and a hundred years when he died.

Numb. 33: 38—39.

And Moses went and spake these words unto all Israel, and said unto them: A son of a hundred and twenty years am I this day.
Deut. 31: 2.

And Moses was a son of a hundred and twenty years when he died.
Deut. 34: 7.

Moses was born in 2457, which is his year 1; and his year 120 is 2576.

Aaron was born in 2454, which is his year 1; and his year 123 is 2576.

Moses died within two months of New Year 2577 (which see), and in year 40 from the Exodus. He thus lived almost 120 **full** years, unless "this day I am a son of 120 years" be pressed to mean his birthday. In any case, he lived 119 full years and at least ten months.

Year 1 in Canaan. **Year 2577.**

And the people came out of the Jordan on **day** ten of the first month [of the New Year after the death of Moses].   Josh. 4: 19.

Caleb 85.   Division of the Land.   **Year 2583.**

And now, behold, I am to-day a son of five and eighty years.—Caleb to Joshua, in asking for a special assignment of his inheritance.
Josh. 14: 10.

Caleb was born in 2498; and 85 are 2583.

Elders die. **Year 2610.**

And Aaron the priest went up at the Lord's commandment to Mount Hor, and died there in year forty from the departure of Israel's children from Egypt land.   Numb. 33: 38.

And they journeyed from Mount Hor . . . . And Israel sent messengers to Sihon king of the Amorites, saying: Let me pass through thy land; . . . but Sihon . . . fought against Israel . . . And Israel took all these cities; and Israel dwelt in all the cities of the Amorites, in Heshbon and all its towns.
Numb. 21: 4, 21—25.

And the people served the Lord all the days of Joshua and all the days of the elders that outlived Joshua . . . And Joshua, son of Nun, the Lord's servant, died . . . and also all that generation were gathered unto their fathers.   Judg. 2: 7—8, 10.

While Israel dwelt in Heshbon and its towns . . . three hundred years, wherefore did ye not recover them?—Jephthah to the Ammon king. Judg. 11: 26.

Hitherto the dates have been obtained from passages of Scripture which furnish a continuous chronology downward from Adam to Year 2583, the Division of the Land under Joshua. Scripture does not give the number of years from this Division to the death of the Elders, or the first Oppression, which is the next **dated** event in Scripture. The date obtainable from the Bible data **downward** next to 2583 is the end of the 300 years spoken of by Jephthah— which began in Year 40 from the Exodus.

There is thus a gap between the Division of the Land and the death of the Elders to be filled in, ere a continuous chronology can be had for the period of the Judges, and this can be done only by working **backward** from the end of Jephthah's 300 years. This gap is found to be of 27 years, thus:

About to end the Ammon oppression of 18 years. Jephthah says to Ammon, Israel dwelt in Heshbon and its towns 300 years. (That this is not to be taken as a round number is shown in Part I § § 68—71). Aaron died in Mount Hor in year 40 from the Exodus. Israel took Heshbon and its town after leaving Mount Hor; therefore, not before that year; and not later: since Moses took it, and he died in the same year as Aaron (see 2576). 300 years and 2576 is 2876, when the Ammon oppression of 18 years ends. It was preceded by 22 years of Jair, 23 of Tola, 3 of Abimelech, 40 "Rest" (see Part I, § 79) associated with Gideon, 40 with Deborah, 80 with Ehud, and 40 with Othniel (see Part 1, § § 77—78), making 266 years. From Year 40 of the Exodus, or 2576, to the Division of the Land in 2583 is 7 years more: 273 years in all (7x13x3). 2583, the year of the Division of the Land, and 273 give 2856 (7x13x24). The 300 years end in 2883, with a difference of 27 years between the two dates. These 27 years cover the time from the Division of the land and the first Oppression (Compare Part I, § § 18—20).

One other long date, covering this period, is given in the Bible: the 480 years from the Exodus to 4 Solomon, when the Temple was begun in 3017 Adam. By working backward therefrom the same result is obtained. But this calculation would have in common with the other the data for the period of the Judges, and would not therefore be an independent line of proof.

40 Years (Othniel's) begin. **Year 2611.**

And the land had rest, forty years.   Judg. 3: 11.

That the Oppressions during the periods of so called "Rest" are included in them is shown in Part I, § § 18—19 and 66—68.

Cushan's Oppression ends. **Year 2618.**

And Israel's sons served Cushan-Rishathaim eight years.

Judg. 3: 8.

As the years of servitude are part of the Rest period (see the preceding year) this Oppression began in 2611, its year 1; and its year 8 is 2618.

40 Year end. Othniel dies. **Year 2650.**

And the land had rest, forty years; and Othniel, son of Kenaz, died. Judg. 3: 11.

The elders died in 2610; and 40 is 2650.

80 Years (Ehud's) begin. **Year 2651.**

And the land had rest, eighty years.   Judg. 3: 30.

As the years of servitude are part of the Rest period (see the preceding year) this Oppression began in 2611, its year 1; and its year 8 is 2618.

Eglon's Oppression ends. **Year 2668.**

And Israel's sons served Eglon king of Moab eighteen years.

Its year 1 being 2651, its year 18 is 2668.   Judg. 3: 14.

80 Years (Ehud's) end.   Ehud dies. **Year 2730.**

And the land had rest, eighty years.   Judg. 3: 30.

Their year 1 being 2651, year 80 is 2730.

The death of Ehud is not mentioned specially; but Judg. 2: 18—19 says expressly: "And when the Lord raised them up judges, then the Lord was with the judge, and saved them out of their enemies' hand all the days of the judge; for it repented the Lord because of their groaning by reason of them that oppressed them and vexed them, but it came to pass WHEN THE JUDGE

WAS DEAD, that they turned back."

40 Years (Deborah's) begin.   Year 2731.

And the land had rest, forty years.   Judg. 5: 31.

Jabin's Oppression ends.   Year 2750.

Jabin, king of Canaan, . . . twenty years he mightily oppressed Israel. Judg. 4: 2—3.

Its year 1 being 2731, year 20 is 2750.

40 Years end.   Deborah dies.   Year 2770.

And the land had rest, forty years.   Judg. 5: 31.

Their year 1 being 2731, year 40 is 2770.

Deborah's death is not expressly mentioned; but her case like Ehud's (see 2730) falls under Judg. 2: 18—19 quoted there.

40 Years (Gideon's) begin.   Year 2771.

And the land had rest, forty years, in Gideon's days.

     Judg. 8:28

Midian Oppression ends.   Year 2777.

And Israel's sons did what was evil in the sight of the Lord, and the Lord delivered them into Midian's hand seven years.

Their year 1 being 2771, year 7 is 2777.   Judg. 6: 1.

40 Years (Gideon's) end, Gideon dies.   Year 2810.

And the land had rest, forty years, in Gideon's days.

     Judg. 8: 28.

And Gideon son of Joash died in a good old age. And it came to pass as soon as Gideon was dead, that Israel's sons turned again and played the harlot after the Baalim.   Judg. 8: 32—33.

This year 1 being 2771, 40 is 2810.

Abimelech's Year 1.   **Year 2811.**

And Abimelech, son of Jerubaal [Gideon], . . . was prince over Israel three years.   Judg. 9: 1, 22.

Abimelech's Year 3, dies.   **Year 2813.**

And a certain woman cast an upper millstone upon Abimelech's head, . . . and he died.   Judg. 9: 53—54.

His year 1 being 2811, 3 is 2813.

Tola's Year 1.   **Year 2814.**

And after Abimelech Tola arose; . . . and he judged Israel twenty-three years, and he died.   Judg. 10: 1—2.

Eli born.   **Year 2830.**

And Eli was a son of ninety and eight years, . . . and he died.

                                                                                                             1 Sam. 4: 15—18.

His year 98 being 2927, which see; his year 1 is 2830.

The Philistine Oppression of 40 years ended with their defeat by Israel's God at Mizpeh in 2947, which see. The ark of God taken at the death of Eli had been in Kiriath Jearim twenty years (1 Sam. 6: 1; 7: 2), when the Oppression ended. Eli died therefore 20 years before 2947, or in 2927.

Tola's Year 23, dies.   **Year 2836.**

His year 1 as Judge, being 2814, 23 is 2836.

Jair's Year 1.   **Year 2837.**

And after him [Tola] arose Jair, . . . and he judged Israel twenty and two years.   Judg. 10: 3.

Jair's Year 22. Dies.   **Year 2858.**

And Jair died.   Judg. 10: 5.

His year 1 being 2837, his year 22 is 2858.

Ammon Oppression end. Year 2876.

Eighteen years oppressed they all the sons of Israel beyond Jordan. Judg. 10: 8.

Jair died in 2858; and 18 are 2876.

That these 300 years begin in 2576, year 40 of the Exodus, is shown in Part I, § 19.

2576 and 300 are 2876.

Jephthah's Year 1. Year 2877.

And Jephthah judged Israel six years; then Jephthah died.

Judg. 12: 7.

Jephthah's Year 6. Dies. Year 2882.

His year 1 being 2877, 6 is 2882.

Ibzan's Year 1. Year 2883.

And after him [Jephthah] Ibzan . . . judged Israel . . . seven years. And Ibzan died. Judg. 12: 8—9.

Eli High-Priest-Judge. Year 2887.

And **Eli** judged Israel forty years. 1 Sam. 4: 18.

Eli was born in 2830, and died in 2927, which years see. 40 years back from his death in 2927 is 2887. He was judge by virtue of his high-priesthood, and could therefore be contemporary with Ibzan, Elon, and Abdon, who were Civil judges only, like all those before Samuel.

Ibzan's Year 7. Dies. Year 2889.

His year 1 being 2883, 7 is 2889.

Elon's Year 1. Year 2890.

And after **Ibzan** Elon . . . judged Israel ten years. And . . . he died. Judg. 12: 11—12.

Elon's Year 10. Dies.   **Year 2899.**

His year 1 being 2890, 10 is 2899.

Abdon's Year 1.   **Year 2900.**

And after **Elon** Abdon . . . judged Israel eight years, and . . . died. Judg. 12: 13—15

Abdon's Year 8. Dies.   **Year 2907.**

His year 1 being 2900, 8 is 2907.

Eli dies, age 98.   **Year 2927.**

Eli was born in 2830 (which see, also 2887); 2830 being his year 1, year 98 is 2927.

Ishbosheth born.   **Year 2935.**

Ishbosheth, Saul's son, was a son for forty years at his reigning over Israel, and he reigned two years.   2 Sam. 2: 10.

He began to reign in 2974, which see. This being his year 40, 1 is 2935. See next date.

David born.   **Year 2944.**

David was a son of thirty years at his reigning, and he reigned forty years.   2 Sam. 5: 4.

From the Exodus in 2537 to the Foundation of Solomon's Temple in year 4 of his reign is 480 years. 4 Solomon is thus 3017 (which see). As David was 70 when he died, these with Solomon's four make 74 years. 3017 is thus David's 74, and his year 1 is 2944.

Both Ishbosheth and David began to reign at Saul's death, so that a date for the one fixes also that of the other.

Philistines 40 Years Oppression end.   **Year 2947.**

And Abdon . . . died . . . . And the Lord delivered them into the Philistines' hands, forty years.   Judg. 12: 15 to 13: 1.

Abdon died 2907 (which see, also 2830); and 40 is 2947.

Mephibosheth born.   **Year 2969.**

Jonathon, Saul's son, had a son lame in his feet; he was a son of five years when tidings came of Saul's and Jonathan's death.

Saul died in 2973, which see. As this was Mephibosheth's year 5, year 1 is 2969.

Samuel dies.   **Year 2971.**

And Samuel judged Israel all the days of his life.

                                                      1 Sam. 7: 15.

David . . . reigned forty years.   2 Sam. 5: 4.

Saul . . . reigned two years over Israel. 1 Sam. 13: 1.

When He had destroyed seven nations in Canaan land, He gave their land for an inheritance for about four hundred and fifty years; and after these **things** He gave judges until prophet Samuel. And afterward they asked **for** a king; and God gave them Saul son of Kish, a man of Benjamin's tribe, for forty years. And when he had removed him, He raised up David to be their king. Paul to the Jews, Acts 13: 19—22.

Solomon's year 4 being 3017, which see, David's year 40 is 3013, and his year 1 is 2974. Saul's 2 years, therefore, are 2972 and 2973. The last year of Samuel's judgeship is thus 2971.

In Part I, § § 12—20, 25, it has been shown that both Canons III and IV demand that the 480 years from Exodus to Temple be held to, in spite of the difficulties presented by Judges and Acts, its apparent dependent. Samuel is clear: The Hebrew, mistranslated here by the Authorized Version, and (though well meaning) falsified by the Revisers, has 1 Sam. 13: 1, A son of one year was Saul at his reigning, and he reigned two years. Verse 2 then goes on, And Saul chose him three thousand men. This is thus the regular, as it were official, account at the beginning of Saul's reign, exactly as given in the case of almost every other king of Judah and Israel. It gives (1) his age when he began to reign; (2) the length of his reign; and then (3) proceeds to the acts of his reign. All is thus here true to form: he was a year old when he began to reign, he reigned two years and did so and so. Intrinsically there is nothing impossible in a babe of one becoming king, dying two years later, and having the acts done in his reign by his regents, guardians, and ministers, attributed to him personally. Standing by themselves, therefore, these two verses offer no reason for tampering with them. The American Revisers have it: Saul was forty (thirty in the English Revision) years old when he began to reign; and when he had reigned two years over Israel Saul chose him three thousand men. The forty they annotate honourably as a conjecture: which, however, has no right at the hands of sinful men in the **text** of God's Holy Book. This false step, however, was presumably taken with the best intentions, though surely under a profound misapprehension as to the needs of the case. But the turn given to the connection between verses 1 and 2 not only mistranslates, it wholly perverts their character, as explained above: setting even an exact date for the choice of the 3000, when the Bible studiously refrains from dating a single one of the numerous incidents of Saul's kingship of some twenty years.

The Revisers, with all others, were led into error here. The Bible narrative itself makes Saul's age of one at his reign impossible; and he lived more than three years, since he had not only a son who died with him in the same battle, he also left a grandson of five. Saul was a son of one year at his reigning, is thus shown from the Bible itself to be a textual error. That it is a primitive error, going back centuries before Christ, is shown by the Seventy, who omit verse 1 altogether, presumably as unintelligible to them in its present form. **They** understood enough of the relation of sinful men to God's Book to bar annotations in the **text**. To confess honestly their ignorance before their patron king here was, from their point of view, impracticable, in their then circumstances. So they left the verse out altogether, thus leaving their silent but convincing witness that (1) the error was as old as their day: and (2) already in their day the means for correcting it were no longer at hand. Numerics rather favour the reading **thirty and one**, instead of the Revisers' unexplained conjecture of forty. But at present our concern is only with the fact that the first half of 1 Sam. 13: 1 is clearly defective; one word, if not two, have been missing therefrom for over two thousand years.

But the presence of an error in the first half has nothing to do with the integrity of its second half, And he reigned two years over Israel.

With the exception of Paul's **apparently** stating in Acts that Saul reigned 40 years (which will presently be shown to be impossible), nothing in the narrative warrants the rejection of the number 2 as the years of Saul's reign for the **purpose of a consecutive Bible Chronology**, WHICH IS INDEED THE CHIEF END OF THE BIBLE DATA BEING GIVEN AT ALL. That Saul was king more than two years, some twenty in fact, is clear from the Bible itself. But the statement, "Samuel judged Israel all the days of his life," forces the meaning that Saul's reign and Samuel's judgeship being contemporaneous, their concurrent years are reckoned chronologically to Samuel, reckoning to Saul only the two years of his sole reign after the death of Samuel.

This account, in accordance with Canon III, Part I, relieves the Bible from the charge of two textual errors where demonstrably there is only one.

Acts 13:19-22 has for centuries been one of the two-three Crosses of Bible Chronologers. Apparently it makes the period from Exodus to Temple thus:

Exodus to Jordan (verse 18)	40 years.
Jordan to Destruction of Nations	x years.
Inheritance	450 years.
Judges until Samuel	x years.
Samuel	x years.
Saul	40 years.
David and Solomon, other sources,	44 years.

The first of the three x periods is known to cover six years. Paul's statement thus accounts for exactly 580 years of the time between Exodus to Temple; and it is probably this result that has caused the wide spread desire among chronologers to change the 480 years of 1 Kings 6: 1 into 580 (See Part I, § § 13—20).

What is here overlooked, however, is this: After the 580 years are thus obtained there still remain the two x periods to be filled in, of which the first alone covers some 300 years only to Jephthah in 2876. From this to Eli's death in 2927 (before which date Samuel's judgeship could not begin) is 51 years more. Thus, even with the third x not yet filled in, the (supposed) 580 years required by Paul's data have already grown to 931, with the end not yet, since x 3 is yet to be heard from.

As competitor with the clear 480 of Kings Paul's statement suffers from two disqualifications: (1) It does not **profess** to be exact: not 450 years, but **about** 450 years; (2) The 950 period being clearly too long by as much as 400 years. and accordingly duly rejected by every worth while chronologer, Paul's statement needs elucidation, and must yield, therefore, to 1 Kings according to Canon IV.

There are at least two plausible explanations of Paul's number 450 for the inheritance of the land. The writer considers indeed neither coercive or final.

But as long as they are possible, no one has a right to assert that there is here a "contradiction" between Paul and the other Bible data.

(1) Some refer the 450 years backward, beginning with the promise to Abraham. To thee HAVE I given this land. This explanation leaves indeed still much to explain. It is neither simple, nor probable, and one that would not readily be thought of. But not being absolutely impossible, or ruled out by the Book itself, it is entitled to be held in reserve as a last **resort**.

(2) Paul's meaning may be: When they got to Canaan God gave it to Israel for an inheritance which was to be for about 450 years. After this (not after the 450 years, but after the destruction of the seven nations just spoken of), He gave them judges. 450 years from the Division of the Land under Joshua in 2583 is 3033, or 20 Solomon. This is within three or four from the end of the 20 years given to the building of the house of God (seven years) and his own house (thirteen years). This difference from the 450 years is covered by Paul's **about**, warning that 450 is only a round number. Did aught occur then that can be taken as an end of the **inheritance** which Paul apparently says was **meant** to last only some 450 years?

At no other time in Israel's history is it recorded, as it is under Solomon, that "Judah and Israel were many as the sand which is by the sea in multitude, eating and drinking and making merry." "And Judah and Israel dwelt safely, every man under his vine and under his fig tree, from Dan even unto Beer Sheba all the days of Solomon" (1 Kings 4: 20, 25).

Here is indeed the full enjoyment by all Israel of their God-given inheritance. But meanwhile aught else came to pass: "Now king Solomon loved many foreign women besides Pharaoh's daughter: women of the Moabites, Ammonites, Edomites, Sidonians, and Hittites: of the nations concerning which the Lord said to Israel's sons, Ye shall not go among them, neither shall they come among you; for surely they will turn away your hearts after their gods. Solomon clave unto these in love. And he had seven hundred wives, princesses, and concubines, and his wives turned away his heart." "And the Lord was angry with Solomon" (1 Kings 11: 1, 5, 9). And Israel's inheritance, henceforth torn in twain, was no longer the one God had originally assigned thereto.

An equally possible and probable variation of this explanation is this: Paul gives three historic events: (1) Wilderness period; (2) Inheritance of land; (3) Judgeship and Saul. To each of these statements is attached a chronological item for a purpose as yet not revealed, but not for a consecutive chronology, as two of the three dates are not definite: the Wilderness is for **about** forty years; the inheritance is for **about** 450 years. Though these two numbers need not be at all consecutive, yet the 40 are not included in the 450; as of saying: In the Wilderness they were about 40 years from the Exodus; then they inherited the land; and this brings us to about 450 years more from the Exodus. Paul is heading all the while for the **seed of David**, and the **establishment** of the kingdom, which is accomplished only by the Lord having at last a **fixed** abode among His people, even the Temple. Now the Temple was finished 487 years from the Exodus. **About** 40 and **about** 450 are **about** 490, which is as near 487 as two **indefinite** numbers can make it.

These three statements moreover cover three periods, each marking a distinct method of the Lord's dealings with His people. With the completion of the Temple a new era began indeed herein for Israel.

The third chronological item, the 40 years, is indeed itself definite enough, but the context is not definite enough to fix the chronology. Not at least until the true interpretation of this passage is assured. It thus falls under Canon IV, and as a less clear datum it cannot affect a result already obtained from indisputably clear data.

As to Paul's apparently assigning to Saul a forty years' reign, exclusive of Samuel's judgeship,—it is impossible. On Saul's death after a supposed reign of forty years David succeeded him at the age of thirty. When David was born Saul has thus been reigning some ten years. Before his meeting with Goliath David had already slain not only bears, but even lions, by simply catching them by the beard. He was thus at least 17, when he slew Goliath, and he may have been two-three years older, as is almost demanded by 1 Sam. 16: 18. An evil spirit from the Lord is troubling the king. His servants urge that a cunning player on the harp be got to drive the spirit away. David is recommended for this purpose thus by one of the king's young men: Behold, I have seen a son of Jesse, cunning in playing, and mighty in valor, and a man of war, and skilled in a matter (or prudent in speech), and a comely man, and the Lord is with him. David is twice here called a man by one who is himself still a young man. A mere royal page would not be the one to recommend the selection of a particular person for a function suggested by others as well as by himself. If the young courtier was even only twenty, David may have also been as much as twenty, if not more.

Now David's victory over Goliath could not have taken place before this his call to court, since the king sends to Jesse (1 Sam. 16: 19), saying, Send me David thy son who is **with the sheep**. Whereas on the day of the victory the king took David "that day, and would let him go no more home to his father's house" (1 Sam. 18: 2). The order of the events of Saul's reign presents indeed serious difficulty, but one thing is clear: If Saul's reign covered full forty years, then at the David-Goliath combat Saul had already been reigning **twenty-seven years**. Saul became jealous of David, because at this victory he heard the women sing, Saul hath slain his thousands and David his ten thousands. From then on David had apparently to keep fleeing for his life from Saul for some **thirteen years**, though this period may be reduced if need be, but at most only by a year or two. But there is nothing in the narrative of Saul's reign suggesting such an abnormal state of affairs.[3]

Again: At the beginning of Saul's reign his son Jonathan is already mature enough to be entrusted with 1000 men out of the 3000 Saul chose for himself, he retaining the other 2000. With his 1000 Jonathan smites the Philistines (1 Sam. 13: 1—3). At the beginning of his father's reign Jonathan is thus an experienced warrior, and is, therefore, at least 20. Saul is, therefore, at least 35 when made king. After a reign of forty years he dies at 75. Considering that at 70 David was already decrepit, Saul at 75 leads his last battle in person, is vigorous enough to endure that Endor trip without food for some 24 hours: to say nothing of his proving a match **at that age** for the

---

3 A chief difficulty in determining the order of events in Saul's reign is: In I Sam. 17: 55—58 David goes forth to meet Goliath, and the king said unto Abner. Whose son is this youth? And Abner said, I know not. And the king said, Inquire whose son the stripling is. And as David returned from the slaughter of the Philistine, Saul said unto him, Whose son art thou, young man? And David answered, I am a son of thy servant Jesse.

David has already been Saul''s harper, the question here has been accepted by all as needing explanation, which however has not been forthcoming, the critics, as usual, making the most thereof. How forsooth could Saul at this time be so ignorant as to his own courtier?

The term **stripling** here need not embarrass as long as David is here called twice a young man. It may have been a sort of love pat in admiration of the departing youth.

As to the question of the king, Saul is not showing here his unacquaintance with **David**, he asks only about his father. This explanation is called "of no importance" by Lange's rationalistic commentator, in the American translation. But this only expressing a state of mind, not giving a reason. In sending for the son of Jesse during his madness, Saul may have easily **afterwards** forgotten about Jesse. Nor must the possibility be excluded of this being a case parallel to that of Pilate in John 19: 7—9. Pilate hears the Jews say that the Lord made himself out to be Son of God. The thought strikes him, What if this be true? He is afraid, and returns to the palace to ask. Whence art thou? David's absolute confidence in his God for victory, the "stripling" going forth unarmed against the giant, the thought **might** suddenly come to Saul, Is here mere man before him? And when Abner does not know who the lad's father is, nothing short of David's own assurance that he is a son of Jesse satisfies the king.

youthful David while chasing him through hill and valley, and forest and swamp. The narrative of Saul's reign does not permit such anomalies.

Once more. One of the two reasons given for Israel's asking for a king is that Samuel becoming old, he made his sons judges, who proved corrupt (1 Sam. 8: 1—5). He might be called old at fifty. But to be old enough to advance this as a reason for withdrawing in part, if indeed not wholly, from his God given ministry, he must have been older, say 55. The sons would not at once display their corruption. Enough time is required for it to be (1) developed; (2) displayed; and (3) to become so notorious in Israel, as to create a political issue of magnitude enough to demand a king. By this time Samuel is surely 60. Not long before Saul's death David is with Samuel (1 Samuel 19: 18). If Saul reigned 40 years, Samuel was well in the nineties when he died. David at 70 is said to be very old (1 Kings 1: 15), and that he died in a good old age full of days (1 Chron. 29: 28). When Eli dies at 98, when Barzillai is 80, the language used about their age is marked. Of Samuel it is merely stated that he died, without any notice of his being in the nineties (1 Sam. 28: 3). When David comes to him Samuel is vigorous enough to move with him to Naioth. Assume that the prophet was about seventy when he died, and all is natural. Let him live to, say, 95, and the whole narrative of his life-time becomes anomalous.

Still, Paul's 40 years would be decisive, if no other meaning could be gotten out of his words. But Paul does not necessarily say just this.

He says, God **gave** them Saul as king for 40 years. In view of the difficulty this statement presents, it is permitted to understand it thus: God's gifts being for final possession always dependent on obedience, He gave the kingdom to Saul for the number of years which in Scripture is the usual number for **testing**. Paul goes on to say, And when He had removed him, He raised up David as king. This phrase is incompatible with the thought that David merely succeeded Saul after his death. Very early in his career was the failure of Saul through disobedience complete, and the Lord told Samuel that He repented Himself of having chosen Saul. He then sent him to anoint David, who did stand the test of obedience. David was anointed accordingly long before Saul's death, and was permitted to reign the full 40 years of test originally designed for his predecessor. This interpretation is confirmed by David's successor, (with whose Temple a new era began for Israel) being also assigned the same number of test for his reign—forty years. The test having failed with Solomon's failure, no other king after him, with one exception, reigns again for 40 years, the number of testing.[4]

One other explanation of Paul's statement is possible, but it is less likely than the one given, and may for the present be therefore omitted. In any case, Saul did not reign 40 years, and yet no disagreement between Paul and the other Bible data is **established**.

Saul's Year 1 — Year 2972.

See the discussion under 2971. Samuel died that year, Saul's year 1 follows the last year of Samuel's judgeship.

Saul's Year 2. Dies. — Year 2973.

His year 1 being 2972, his year 2 is 2973.

David's Year 1. Ishbosheth's 1. — Year 2974.

David succeeded Saul in the kingdom. "And when He had removed him (Saul), He raised up David to be their king (Acts 13: 22). Saul's reign ended in 2973. See 2971, 2980, and 3013, also Part 1 § 69; also next year.

Ishbosheth's Year 2. — Year 2975.

Now Abner, son of Ner, captain of Saul's host, had taken Ishbosheth, Saul's son, and brought him to Mahanaim; and he made him king over

---

4 It is the nature of Light that where it does not enlighten, it darkens. The light once brought to him, never leaves one the same as before. If not left the better for it, he is now much the worse. He who Himself is the Light of the world was set for the falling as well as for the rising of many even in Israel. And he to whom the Redeemer is not the Rock of salvation, knows Him only as a rock of offence and a stone of stumbling. And as the Word of Truth and the sons of Truth are an integral part of Him who is the Truth, they are in like case with Him. Accordingly, this threefold successive use here of a reign of forty years has particularly stumbled the children of darkness.

But historicity has ways of its own, and keeps going down the ages with its stern, but oft staggeringly freakish **facts** and this without waiting with their appearance for the leave of the critics. Thus of the three French dynasties that preceded that of Napoleon, every one ended with three brothers reigning in succession. The Bourbons ended with Louis XVI and his two brothers Louis XVIII, and Charles X. The house of Valois that preceded it ended with Charles Francis II and Henry III, again three brothers. And the dynasty before the Valois ended likewise. Yet no historian has ever seen here aught but plain matters of fact, least of all the sinister artificialities, so readily found by the Critics in the Bible. It is a divine mockery upon the Critics that this very thrice forty which stumbled them so is a most instructive numeric parable that almost cries out, Stop, Look, Listen, and you will surely learn aught.

Gilead, and over the Ashurites, and over Jezreel, and over Ephraim, and over Benjamin, and over all Israel. Ishbosheth, son of Saul, was a son of forty years at his reigning, and he reigned two years. But the house of Judah followed David. And the time that David was king in Hebron over the house of Judah was seven years and six months.

2 Samuel 2: 8—11

Ishbosheth's year 1 being 2874, 2 is 2975.

David's Year 7 — Year 2980.

David was a son of thirty years at his reigning, and he reigned forty years. In Hebron he reigned over Judah seven years and six months; and in Jerusalem he reigned thirty and three years over all Israel and Judah. 2 Sam. 5: 4—5.

His year 1 being 2974, 7 is 2980.

David's Year 40, Dies. — Year 3013.

And David slept with his fathers, and was buried in David's city. And the days that David reigned over Israel were forty years: seven years reigned he in Hebron, and thirty and three years reigned he in Jerusalem. 1 Kings 2: 10—11.

His year 1 being 2974, 40 is 3013.

Solomon's Year 1. — Year 3014.

And Solomon sat upon the throne of David his father.

1 Kings 2: 12.

Solomon's Year 3. Shimei dies. — Year 3016.

And Shimei dwelt in Jerusalem. And it came to pass that at the end of three years, that two of Shimei's servants ran away.

1 Kings 2: 39.

Solomon's year 1 being 3014, 3 is 3016.

At David's request Solomon was to punish Shimei for reviling him during his flight from Absalom. In year 1 of his reign Solomon forbade Simeon to leave Jerusalem on pain of death. On returning to the City with his fugitives, he was put to death (1 Kings 2: 8—9; 39—46).

Solomon's Year 4. Temple began.   Year 3017.

And it came to pass in eighty years and four hundred years from the departure of Israel's children, from Egypt land in the fourth year . . . of Solomon's reign, and he began to build the house of the Lord. 1 Kings 6: 1.

The Exodus was in 2537; and 480 is 3017.

11 Solomon.   Year 3024.

And in the year eleven . . . was the house finished . . . And he was seven years in building it.   1 Kings 6: 18.

1 Solomon being 3014; his year 11 is 3024.

24 Solomon.   Year 3037.

And his house Solomon was building thirteen years, and he finished all his house.   1 Kings 7: 1.

And it came to pass at the end of twenty years wherein Solomon had built the two houses, the Lord's house and the king's house. 1 Kings 9:10.

The Temple was begun in 3017; and 20 is 3037

40 Solomon. Dies.   Year 3053.

And the days which Solomon reigned over all Israel in Jerusalem were forty year.   1 Kings 11: 42.

His year 1 being 3014, 40 is 3053.

1 Rehoboam. 1 Jeroboam.   Year 3054.

And Solomon slept with his fathers, and Rehoboam his son reigned in his stead.   1 Kings 11:43.

And Israel revolted from David's house unto this day. And it came to pass when all Israel heard that Jeroboam was returned, that they sent and called him unto the Congregation, and made him king over all Israel. None was behind David's house save Judah only. 1 Kings 12: 20.

3 Rehoboam.   **Year 3056.**

And they strengthened Judah's kingdom and made Rehoboam, Solomon's son, strong for three years; for they walked in David's way and Solomon's for three years.

                                                                                                  2 Chron. 11: 17.

His year 1 being 3054, his year 3 is 3056.

5 Rehoboam.   **Year 3058.**

And it was in the fifth year of king Rehoboam that Shishak king of Egypt came up against Jerusalem.

                                                1 Kings 14: 25; 2 Chron. 12: 2.

1 Rehoboam being 3056, 5 is 3058.

17 Rehoboam; dies.   **Year 3070.**

A son of forty and one years was Rehoboam at his reigning, and seventeen years reigned he in Jerusalem.   1 Kings 14: 21.

His year 1 being 3054, 17 is 3070.

To be 21 in 3054, he was born in 3013. This year is already entered as year 40 of David.

1 Abijam; 18 Jeroboam.   **Year 3071.**

And in year eighteen of king Jeroboam son of Nebat Abijam reigned over Judah. Three years he reigned.   1 Kings 15: 1—2.

1 Jeroboam being 3054, 18 is 3071.

3 Abijam, dies; **20 Jeroboam.**   **Year 3073.**

See year 3071. 1 Abijam being 3071, 3 is 3073.

1 Asa.   **Year 3074.**

And Abijam slept with his fathers, and Asa his son reigned in his stead. 1 Kings 15: 8.

2 Asa. 1 Nadab.   **Year 3075.**

And Nadab, son of Jeroboam, reigned over Israel in year two of Asa king of Judah, and he reigned over Israel two years.

1 Kings 15: 25.

See for some of the kings of **Israel** not being FULL years, Part I, § § 82—83.

3 Asa. 2 Nadab, dies.   **Year 3076.**

In year three of Asa king of Judah Baasha slew him (Nadab), and reigned in his stead.

In year three of Asa King of Judah Baasha, son of Ahijah, reigned over all Israel in Tirzah—twenty-four years.

1 Kings 15: 28, 33.

Compare also Part I, § § 82—83.

1 Asa being 3074, 3 is 3076.

Jehoshaphat born.   **Year 3080.**

Jehoshaphat was a son of thirty-five years at his reigning.

1 Kings 22: 42

1 Jehoshaphat is 3115, which see. He died after reigning twenty-five years, in 3139, which see. He could be "a son of thirty-five years" also if born in 3081, and 3115 would then be his year 35. But he began to reign "in year four of Ahab" (verse 41), which is the year his father Asa died in. Jehoshaphat was thus 35 not in his first regnal year, but in the year in which his actual reign began, though reckoned to his father's reign. To be 35 in 3115 **thus**, he must be born in 3080. Born in 3081, he would only be 34 in the year of his father's death.

10 Asa.   **Year 3083.**

Asa reigned. In his days the land was quiet ten years.

2 Chron. 14: 1.

15 Asa.   **Year 3088.**

And they assembled at Jerusalem in the third month of year fifteen of Asa's reign.   2 Chron. 15: 10.

1 Asa is 3074; 15 is 3088.

26 Asa; 24 Baasha, dies; 1 Elah.   **Year 3099.**

In year three of Asa king of Judah Baasha, son of Abijah, reigned over all Israel in Tirzah, twenty and four years.

1 Kings 15: 33.

In year twenty and six of Asa king of Judah Elah son of Baasha reigned over Israel in Tirzah, two years.   1 Kings 16: 8.

As 1 Asa is 3074, 26 Asa is 3099. As 1 Baasha is 3076, 24 Baasha is also 3009. 24 Baasha and 1 Elah are therefore not two separate years, as is invariably the case with the similar data of the kings of Judah, but one year.

27 Asa, 2 Elah, dies. **1 Omri.**   **Year 3100.**

In year twenty and seven of Asa king of Judah Zimri came and smote him [Elah], and reigned in his stead seven days in Tirzah. And the people made Omri, captain of the host, king over Israel. 1 Kings 16: 10, 15, 16.

31 Asa. 5 Omri. Tibni dies.   **Year 3104.**

The people of Israel were divided into two parts: half of the[1] people followed Tibni, and half followed Omri. And the people that followed Omri prevailed against the people that followed Tibni. And Tibni died. 1 Kings 16: 21—22.

In year 31 of Asa king of Juda Omri reigned over Israel—twelve years. In Tirzah he reigned six years.   1 Kings 16: 23.

1 Omri is Year 3100, and 27 Asa; 31 Asa is thus 5 Omri, and 1 Kings 16: 23 can only mean that in 31 Asa Omri became **undisputed** king on Tibni's death. But his whole reign from Zimri's death was 12 years. See 3105 and 3111.

6 Omri.   **Year 3105.**

In Tirzah he [Omri] reigned six years.   1 Kings 16: 23.

1 Omri being 3100, 6 Omri is 3105.

---

1 Typographical error corrected from the 1950 edition; "of the" had been rendered "he".

35 Asa. Jehoram born.   **Year 3108.**

Jehoram, son of Jehoshaphat king of Judah reigned. A son of thirty and two years he was at his reigning, and eight years he reigned in Jerusalem. 2 Kings 8: 16—17.

1 Jehoram is 3140, which see; 8 Jehoram is 3147, which see; to be 32 in 3140, and reign 8 years, he must be born in 3108.

[36 Asa.]   **[Year 3109.]**

And there was no war till year thirty and five of Asa's reign. In year thirty and six of Asa's reign (kingdom?) Baasha king of Israel went up against Judah.   2 Chron. 15: 19 to 16: 1.

Baasha died in 3099, 10 years before 3109. 1 Kings 15: 32 says, And there was war between Asa and Baasha **all their days**. The statement therefore that there was no war till 35 Asa, and Baasha went up against Judah, needs clearing up. 35 Asa, Year 3108, is already entered, because Jehoram his son was born therein, and concerns us at present no further. But 36 Asa cannot be entered under the circumstances. The choice is between a primitive copyist's error either about the year, or about the name Baasha (which, however, remain unidentified), and the explanation that Year 36 of Asa's reign, stands for year 36 of Judah's kingdom. This would throw it back to 16 Asa, thus: Rehoboam's 17 years, Abijam's 3, and Asa's 16 make 36 years for the kingdom of Judah. The word for reign, **malcuth**, means also kingdom. But this would be the only instance of this meaning of the word in such a connection, among its numerous occurrences, and would not be thought of except in a desperate case like this.

Whatever the explanation of the difficulty, the year 3109, though expressly named in the Book, cannot now be entered as yet, Numerics also being against it, as is shown in Part III. On the other hand, the interpretation that calls in here 16 Asa, with 3089 thus becoming a candidate for the List, is a mere human guess, without any Bible data to support its admission. It too, therefore, must for the present be rejected. See also Part I, § 24.

38 Asa. 12 Omri, dies.   **Year 3111.**

Ahab's accession.

And Omri slept with his fathers . . . and Ahab his son reigned in his stead.

And Ahab, Omri's son, reigned over Israel in year thirty and eight years of Asa king of Judah.   1 Kings 16: 28—29.

Ahab succeeded Omri. 1 Omri being 3100, 12 Omri is 3111.

41 Asa, dies; 3 Ahab.   Year 3114.

And Asa slept with his fathers, and died in year forty and one of his reign.   2 Chron. 16: 13.

1 Asa being 3074, his 41 is 3114.

1 Jehoshaphat; 4 Ahab.   Year 3115.

And Jehoshaphat his (Asa's) son reigned in his stead.

2 Chron. 17: 1.

And Jehoshaphat, Asa's son, reigned over Judah in year four of Ahab king of Israel.   1 Kings 22: 41.

1 Ahab being 3112, 4 Ahab is 3115.

3 Jehoshaphat.   Year 3117.

And in year three of his reign **Jehoshaphat** sent his princes to teach in the cities of Judah.   2 Chron. 17: 7.

1 Jehoshaphat being 3115, 3 is 3117.

Ahaziah born.   Year 3126.

A son of twenty and two years Ahaziah was at his reigning, and he reigned on year in Jerusalem.   2 Kings 8: 26.

A son of forty and two years was Ahaziah at his reigning.

2 Chron. 22: 2.

The year of Ahaziah's reign was 3148, which see; he was thus 23 when he died. His year 23 being 3148, his year 1 is 3126.

This according to Kings, which makes him 22 where Chronicles makes him forty and two. These two statements thus need to be reconciled.

Ahaziah's father was Jehoram, of whom 2 Chron. 21:5 says that he was a son of thirty and two years at his reigning, and he reigned eight years. This is repeated in verse 20: A son of thirty and two years he was at his reigning, and he reigned eight years. This is confirmed in 2 Kings 8: 17: A son of thirty and two years he was at his reign, and eight years he reigned.

If Jehoram died at the end of his reign, he was then 40 at most, and his son could not be his successor at 42, unless there was a long interval between the death of the father and the accession of the son. Of such an interval no intimation is given, and without a knowledge of its length a consecutive chronology becomes thereafter impossible.

Did Jehoram then live some years after his reign, as did perhaps Jotham? This might account for his son being 42 at his reign, but the fatal gap remains. Moreover, the record here is complete. 2 Kings 8: 25 says that he was buried with his fathers, and Ahaziah his son reigned in his stead. This language demands no interval. Ahaziah's father thus dying at 40, the son could not then be 42. Chronicles is thus clearly shown to contain a copyist's error.

In Part III Numerics show Ahaziah's true age here to be 22, and not 42.

17 Jehoshaphat.   **Year 3131.**

Ahaziah, son of Ahab, reigned over Israel in Samaria in year seventeen of Jehoshaphat king of Judah—two years.

1 Kings 22: 51.

1 Jehoshaphat being 3115, his 17 is 3131.

The synchronism of 1 Ahaziah with 17 Jehoshaphat, needs clearing up, as it disagrees with other clear data for these reigns. Ahab, Ahaziah's father, reigned 22 years, and these reach to 3133, which see; but this is 19 Jehoshaphat. His successor's sole reign cannot, therefore, begin in 17 Jehoshaphat. two years before his father's death. If, therefore, he is found reigning in 17 Jehoshaphat, it can only mean that in Ahab's years 20, 21, 22 corresponding to Jehoshaphat's 17, 18, 19, the son was either regent for his father, or reigned with him.

Under year 3132 it is seen that though Ahab and his son Ahaziah are already reigning together, Jehoram, another son of Ahab, begins then to reign also. This makes three persons reign at the same time over Israel in Ahab's life time: an unusual, but not impossible, nor even an improbable condition for those turbulent times in Israel. As no error in the text is to be assumed as long as a rational explanation is possible, it is only necessary here to suppose this: Two years before his death, either because away at war or already failing, Ahab appoints Ahaziah as his successor and his fellow ruler. After a year Ahaziah, who lives only one year longer, is found to be too sickly to rule, or otherwise incapacitated. Jehoram, therefore, his other son, is appointed by Ahab as successor to Ahaziah, and fellow-ruler with him, and thus Jehoram also "reigns" in 3132, even though his father and brother are both still alive and reigning. See also 3136, and Part I, § 89.

18 Jehoshaphat.   Year 3132.

And Jehoram, Ahab's son, reigned over Israel in Samaria in year 18 of Jehoshaphat king of Judah, and he reigned twelve years. 2 Kings 3: 1.

See Year 3131.

1 Jehoshaphat being 3115, his 18 is 3132.

22 Ahab; 19 Jehoshaphat.   Year 3133.

Ahab, Omri's son, reigned over Israel twenty and two years.

1 Kings 16: 29.

1 Ahab being 3112, his year 22 is 3133.

1 Ahaziah of Israel. 20 Jehoshaphat.   Year 3134.

Ahaziah, Ahab's son, reigned two years over Israel

1 Kings 22: 51.

As Ahab reigned 22 years, extending to 19 Jehoshaphat, 1 Ahaziah is 20 Jehoshaphat, and is not therefore 17 Jehoshaphat, or year 3131, which see.

2 Ahaziah of Israel. Dies.   Year 3135.

Ahaziah reigned two years.   1 Kings 22: 51.

1 Jehoram of Israel; 22 Jehoshophat.   Year 3136.

And Jehoram reigned in **Ahaziah's** stead in year two of Jehoram, son of Jehoshaphat king of Judah.   2 Kings 1:17.

And Jehoram, Ahab's son, reigned in year eighteen of Jehoshaphat. 2 Kings 3: 1.

Under years 3147, 3148, it is seen that this Jehoram of Israel dies at the same time with Ahaziah of Judah in 3148, thus filling up his 12 years: the twelfth falling also in the last year of Ahaziah's brother and predecessor, Jehoram of Judah. 1 Jehoram of Israel is therefore, 3136, which is 22 Jehoshaphat. It cannot, therefore, be year 18 of Jehoshaphat, as given in 2 Kings 3: 1; nor in 2 Jehoram of Judah, which 3141. The adjustment of these and all similar difficulties is found below in the Table of the Kings of Judah and Israel. Compare Part 1, Section 89 and year 3131 above.

25 Jehoshaphat.   Year 3139.

And Jehoshaphat reigned twenty and five years.

1 Kings 22: 42.

1 Jehoshaphat being 3115, his 25 is 3139.

1 Jehoram; 5 Jehoram of Israel.   Year 3140.

In year five of Joram, son of Ahab king of Israel, Jehoshaphat being then king of Judah, Jehoram, son of Jehoshaphat, king of Judah, reigned. 2 Kings 8: 16.

1 Joram being 3136, 5 Joram is 3140. And as the last year of Jehoshaphat is 3139, his successor Jehoram's year 1 is also 3140.

The words **Jehoshaphat being then king of Judah** have stumbled the enemies of the Bible, perplexed its friends, and puzzled some of the ancient versions. The versions express their embarrassment by omitting the sentence, as if not knowing what to make thereof. The friendly commentators frankly confess their helplessness here. And the critics point to another "contradiction." Jehoshaphat, forsooth, alive in the reign of the **two** Jehorams, his reign moreover having ended the year before. The suave, however, are content with the still equally destructive dictum of the text being here "corrupt."

For a **consecutive** Chronology the reigns of rulers cannot be reckoned in their exact length, since only presidents of republics, and other like elected officials, have their terms of office begin and end on fixed dates. Otherwise it is with hereditary rulers. Their times and seasons being appointed by the Most High, who alone lifteth up and casteth down, the calendar of Heaven is not necessarily Egyptian, Julian, or Gregorian. Such rulers are clearly not ordained to rule each a fixed term, say, from January to January. But for the purpose of an earthly consecutive chronology this is exactly the way a reign must be reckoned. A king may reign any number of days in the year, from 365 to only one, the whole of the last year of a king's reign is usually assigned him. If a king dies in the first month of the year, that year is usually reckoned as of his reign, though this successor had eleven months thereof. Without some such fixed rule no systematic, consecutive chronology is possible. And with this rule rigidly followed in the case of the kings of Judah (whose date alone are meant to furnish a continuous chronology, see Part I, §§ 84—85), there is, accordingly order and harmony throughout.

For reasons, however, which the Spirit has not deemed best to give, He has thought it fit to break this rule in the one case of Jehoshaphat, who clearly was meant to be assigned 25 years of reign, and yet was alive in the twenty-sixth, which was not designed to be reckoned as his. **Of this departure from the rule the words,** Jehoshaphat being then king of Judah, **are an effective as well as special warning** that in this case that rule was not being followed.

2 Jehoram.   Year 3141.

And Joram [of Israel] reigned in year two of Jehoram [of Judah]. 2 Kings 1: 17.

Under 3140 it is seen that 1 Jehoram is 5 Joram; 2 Jehoram should therefore be 6 Joram, while here it is 1 Joram. This, and the several other like cases among the kings of Israel are all accounted for in the same manner according to Canon VIII. Though no joint reigns are specifically named in such cases, their data demand, and are explained by, them as is seen in the Table for the kings of Judah and Israel at the end of this Part. See also Part I, § 89.

6 Jehoram.   Year 3145.

And it came to pass unto days from days, and as at the going out of the time of the end of days, two, his bowels fell out by reason of sickness, and he [Jehoram] died.   2 Chron. 21: 19.

This confessedly obscure datum is given by the Revisers as, In process of time at the end of two years. As Jehoram reigned 8 years and died in 2137, which see, two years before is 3145.

This is the only year in Bible Chronology entered here not from a direct statement of the text, but from its—interpretation. The expression, The time of the going out of the end of days, two, is taken by commentators to mean here two years, but Keil takes it as days. The Seventy do not render it as year, but their English translators say that it **must** mean year, and so render it. **Days** gives a sense at best very problematic, and the mention of the sickness almost compels the rendering **year**, which in the phrase itself is allowable enough, provided dogmatism is left here without. Numerics, however, which have already settled not a few interpretations, decide here for **years**, as is seen in part III.

8 Jehoram, dies.   Year 3147.

Jehoram reigned 8 years.   2 Kings 8: 17.

1 Jehoram being 3140, his year 8 is 3147.

1 Ahaziah, dies. Joash born.   Year 3148.

Jehoram of Israel dies.

And Jehoram slept with his fathers, and his son Ahaziah reigned in his stead. In year twelve years of Joram, son of Ahab, king of Israel, Ahaziah, son of Jehoram, reigned over Judah. A son of twenty and two years was Ahaziah at his reigning, and he reigned one year. 2 Kings 8: 24—25.

And Jehoram, Ahab's son, reigned over Israel twelve years.

2 Kings 3: 1.

And Joram king of Israel and Ahaziah king of Judah went out to meet Jehu. And Jehu drew his bow with his full strength, and smote Joram between his arms, and the arrow went out at his heart. When Ahaziah king of Judah saw this his fled. And Jehu followed after him and said, Smite him also in the chariot. And he fled to Megiddo and died there.   2 Kings 9: 21—27.

Jehoash was a son of seven years at his reigning. In year seven of Jehu reigned Jehoash, and he reigned forty years.[1]

---

1 No single exception does of itself necessarily invalidate a conclusion drawn from the case in general. In this case however, the exception may be only apparent. Both kings, of Israel and Judah, are slain by Jehu. The royal house of Israel is wiped out by Jehu; that of Judah by Athaliah. Joash is saved only by being stolen away when a babe of scarcely a year, and is hid for six years. In all these years only this young forfeited life stood between the fulfilment of the promise to David concerning the fruit of his loins, the Messiah. It is very likely (though nothing thereof is recorded) that at this clearly national crisis of the people of God, extending as it does to both kingdoms, the babe was specially preserved for giving Judah at least another start, another—**test**. If this be the case, Joash

2 Kings 12: 1.

As 1 Jehoram was 3136, he reigned twelve full years, being slain by Jehu at the same time with Ahaziah.

As Joash began to reign in 3155, and was already born when his brothers were slain by Athaliah, he was born not later than 3148, and was thus full seven in 3155, year 1 of his reign.

1 Athaliah. 1 Jehu.   **Year 3149.**

He [Ahaziah] fled to Megiddo, and died there.   2 Kings 9: 27

And Athaliah was Ahaziah's mother; and she saw that her son was dead, and she arose and destroyed all the seed royal. And Jehosheba, daughter of king Joram, sister of Ahaziah, took Joash, Ahaziah's son, and stole him away from among the king's sons that were slain, him and his nurse, in the chamber of beds; and they hid him from Athaliah's face, and he was not slain. And he was with her hid in the house of the Lord six years; and Athaliah reigned over the land.   2 Kings 11: 1—3.

6 Athaliah.   **Year 3154.**

And Athaliah reigned over the land. And in the seventh year she was slain.   2 Kings 11: 3, 16.

As Joash was hid six years, they cover Athaliah's reign. Her year 1 being 3149, 6 is 3154.

1 Joash, 7 Jehu.   **Year 3155.**

Jehoash was a son of seven years in his reigning. In year seven of Jehu Jehoash reigned.   2 Kings 12: 1.

1 Jehu being 3149, his year 7 is 3155.

Amaziah born.   **Year 3170.**

In year two of Joash, son of Jehoahaz, king of Israel, Amaziah son of Joash king of Judah reigned. He was a son of twenty and five years at his reign,   and   he   reigned   twenty   and   nine   years. 2 Kings 14: 1.

---

is the only other king who could with propriety be assigned for his reign exactly forty years, the special number of testing.

1 Amaziah is 3195, which see; his reign ended in 3223, which see. He was thus 25 at his reign, and 53 at its end; thus born in 3170.

28 Jehu.   **Year 3176.**

And the days which Jehu reigned over Israel were twenty and eight years. 2 Kings 10: 36.

His year 1 being 3149, his year 28 is 3176.

23 Joash. 1 Jehoahaz.   **Year 3177.**

In year twenty and three of Joash son of Ahaziah king of Judah Jehoahaz, son of Jehu, reigned over Israel, seventeen years. 2 Kings 13: 1.

1 Joash being 3155, his year 23 is 3177.

This datum furnishes an illustration of what God's Book has to undergo at the hands not only of its enemies but even its—friends.

2 Kings 12:1 says: A son of seven years was Jehoash at his reign. In Jehu's year seven Jehoash reigned. If 1 Jehoash is 7 Jehu, the difference between the two reigns in years is six.

In 2 Kings 13:1, Jehu's son Ahaziah reigns in 23 Jehoash. If 1 Jehoash is 7 Jehu, his 23 is 22 years later, or 29 Jehu; and the difference between 23 and 29 is the same—six.

But 23 Jehoash is here not 29 Jehu, but 1 Ahaziah. This evidently means that Jehu's reign was only 28 years, and what would have been his year 29 is year 1 of his successor, and the same 23 Joash. Accordingly 2 Kings 10: 36 definitely says, And the days which Jehu reigned over Israel were twenty and eight years. These three statements are thus as harmonious as arithmetic can make them; thus:

```
 1 Jehoash       is  7 Jehu.
22 Jehoash       is 28 Jehu, dies.
23 Jehoash       is 29 Jehu, or 1 Jehoahaaz.
```

And now for the commentator on 2 Kings 13:1, Bishop Patrick, sane, judicious, and ever boldly facing the difficulties not infrequent in Holy Writ. Says he:

"Some have raised a doubt about this account because Joash began to reign in the seventh year of Jehu (2 Kings 12: 1), who reigned only 28 years (2 Kings 10: 36); whence if seven years be deducted, there remain no more than one and twenty, and not three and twenty as it is here said. To which Kimchi and Abarbanel answer there were two incomplete years; for when it is said Joash reigned in the seventh year of Jehu, it must be understood of the beginning of the seventh year: and in like manner when he speaks here of the three and twentieth year of Joash. it must be understood of the beginning of the same year. But it is better to say (as my worthy friend Dr. Alix thinks) that there is an interregnum of a year between the death of Jehu and the first of Jehoahaz."

Here are two celebrated Jewish commentators, an Anglican bishop of justly high repute, with a presumably competent Dr. Alix, all inventing a gap of two years that is not a gap; and one even finding an "interregnum."

37 Joash. 1 Joash, of Israel, joint.   **Year 3191.**

In year thirty and seven of Joash king of Judah Jehoash son of Jehoahaz reigned over Israel in Samaria, sixteen years.

2 Kings 13: 10.

1 Joash being in 3155, his year 37 is 3191.

Under 3177 it is seen that Jehoahaz reigned 17 years. His 1 being 3177, his year 17 is 3193. His son and successor Jehoash could not therefore begin his **sole** reign in 3191. This therefore is a case of a joint reign of Jehoahaz either with his son or with his father. If his father, his son's year 1 **would** be 3191. But under 3195, which see, it is shown that 1 Joash sole reign is 3194, and not 3191.

39 Joash.   17 Jehoahaz.   Zechariah dies.   **Year 3193.**

See year 3177, which being 1 Jehoahaz, his year 17 is 3193. And 1 Joash being 3155, his year 38 is also 3193.

40 Joash, dies.   **1 Joash, of Israel,** sole.   **Year 3194.**

Jehoash was a son of seven years at his reign. In year seven of Jehu Joash reigned, and forty years he reigned.   2 Kings 12: 1.

1 Joash being 3155, his year 40 is 3194. See also the Note on page 113.

1 Amaziah.   2 Joash, of Israel. **Year 3195.**

In year two of Joash son of Joahaz king of Israel Amaziah son of Joash, king of Judah, reigned. A son of twenty and five years was he at his reign, and he reigned twenty and nine years.

2 Kings 14: 1.

Amaziah succeeded his father Joash, whose reign ended in 3194. His own year 1 is thus 3195. This year being expressly named as 2 Joash of Israel, his year 1 is 3194; and 3193 is thus year 17, the last, of his father Jehoahaz. The joint reign discussed under 3191 is, therefore, that of Jehoahaz with his son, and not with his father.

1 Jeroboam, joint. **Year 3198.**

In year twenty and seven years of Jeroboam king of Israel reigned Azariah son of Amaziah.   2 Kings 15: 1.

Under year 3224, which see, it is shown that it is 1 Azariah. If 3224 is year 27 of Jeroboam, his year 1 is 3198.

Under 3209, which see, it is shown that Jeroboam then also began his reign, which therefore is his sole reign. In 3198, therefore, only his joint reign begins.

Azariah born. **Year 3208.**

A son of sixteen years was **Azariah** at his reign.

2 Kings 15: 2; 2 Chron. 26: 3.

And all the people took Azariah (and he be a son of sixteen years), and made him king in place of his father Amaziah.

2 Kings 14: 21.

1 Azariah being 3224, which see, he being then 16, 3224 less 16 is 3208.

15 Amaziah. 16 Joash, dies. **1 Jeroboam,** sole. **Year 3209.**

Amaziah lived after the death of Jehoash, son of Jehoahaz, fifteen years. 2 Kings 14: 17.

In year fifteen of Amaziah Jeroboam reigned in Samaria, forty and one years.   2 Kings 14: 23.

Under 3223, which see, it is shown that Amaziah reigned 29 years; and 3223 being his year 29, his year 15 is 3209.

Under 3198 Jeroboam's reign is also seen to begin. It had thus two beginnings: of his joint, and of his sole reign.

29 Amaziah, dies.   **Year 3223.**

Amaziah reigned twenty and nine years. And they made a conspiracy against him and slew him.   2 Kings 14: 2, 19.

1 Amaziah being 3195, his year 29 is 3223.

1 Amaziah (Uzziah).   27 Jeroboam, joint.   **Year 3224.**

And they brought him [Amaziah] upon the horses, and he was buried with his fathers in David's city. And all the people took Azariah, and made him king in his father's place.

2 Kings 14: 20—21.

3223 being Amaziah's last, 1 Azariah (his successor's) is the following year 3224.

In year twenty and seven years of Jeroboam king of Israel reigned Azariah.   2 Kings 15: 1.

As Jeroboam's sole reign began in 3209, this his year 27 is that of his joint reign. Its year 1 being 3198, his 27 is 3224.

41 Jeroboam, joint.   **Year 3238.**

In year fifteen years of Amaziah Jeroboam reigned, forty and one years. 2 Kings 14: 23.

These 41 years cannot mean his sole reign, which began only in 3209. His joint reign began in 3198, which being his year 1, his year 41 is 3238. To push these 41 years down 11 years, to make them his sole reign is to dislocate several synchronisms of the kings of Judah and Israel.

Jotham born.   **Year 3251.**

A son of five and twenty years Jotham was at his reign.

2 Kings 15: 33.

1 Jotham is 3276, which see. He is then 25. 3276 less 25 is 3251.

38 Azariah.   1 Zechariah.   **Year 3261.**

In year thirty and eight years of Azariah Zechariah reigned over Israel. 2 Kings 15: 8.

3224 being year 1 of Azariah, his year 38 is 3261.

For the years 3239—3260, a period of 22 years, there is no record of a king in Israel. Commentators and chronologers accept here the easy and every ready at hand expedient of an "interregnum" of which frequent and needless use is made by them (compare Year 3177). There may have been no interregnum at all. The data of the kings of Israel are not being given for the purpose of a consecutive Chronology (those of Judah alone being given for this end), the Blessed Holy Spirit may have deemed it best to pass over the names of the king or kings for those 22 years, just as He has passed over four of the kings of Judah in the genealogy of Matt. 1: 1—7. Anstey's charge of a great "blot" against Archbishop Usher (of blessed memory) for not adding 11 years more to such fanciful interregna is thus a melancholy example of the length to which even well-meaning folk will be carried by their own theorizings.

But even if this be an interregnum, this would be the only interregnum at al deducible from the data of Scripture itself. All the others are at best problematic.

19 Azariah. 1 Shallum. Menahem's accession.   **Year 3262.**

Shallum reigned in year thirty and nine years of Uzziah [Azariah] king of Judah.   2 Kings 15: 13.

In year thirty and nine years of Azariah reigned Menahem.

                                                                2 Kings 15: 17.

1 Uzziah being 3224, his year 39 is 3262.

Ahaz born.   10 Menahem.   **Year 3272.**

A son of twenty years was Ahaz at his reign.   2 Kings 16: 2.

In year thirty and nine years of Azariah Menahem reigned over Israel, ten years.   2 Kings 15: 17.

1 Ahaz is 3292, which see; less 20 is 3272.

Menahem began to reign in 39 Azariah, or 3262; and 10 is 3272.

50 Azariah.   1 Pekaiah.   **Year 3273.**

In year fifty years of Azariah Pekaiah reigned over Israel, two years. 2 Kings 15: 23.

1 Azariah being 3224, his year 50 is 3273.

51 Azariah.   2 Pekaiah.   **Year 3274.**

See the year preceding, which is 1 Pekaiah.

52 Azariah.   1 Pekah.   **Year 3275.**

In year fifty and two years of Azariah Pekah son of Remaliah reigned over Israel, twenty years.   2 Kings 15: 27.

1 Azariah being 3224, his year 52 is 3275.

1 Jotham.   2 Pekah.   **Year 3276.**

In year two of Pekah Jotham reigned.   2 Kings 15: 32.

See the year preceding, which is 1 Pekah.

Hezekiah born.   **Year 3283.**

A son of twenty and five years was he [Hezekiah] at his reigning. 2 Kings 18: 2.

His year 1 is 3308, which see, less 25 is 3283.

At Hezekiah's birth his father Ahaz is 11 years old. The well-intentioned commentators endeavour here to steady the Ark, and strenuously lay out poor Ahaz on their Procrustes bed, and think they are doing the great God a service, if they lengthen the father's age to at least 14. A merciful God has refrained from making a breach upon them as upon Uzzah of old. He has not spared them from making here a breach upon his Word. See Part I, § 90, where this case is discussed; also that of king Josiah, who at **eight** began to seek after the Lord, and began at twelve a great religious Revival throughout his kingdom.

16 Jotham, dies.   **17 Pekah.**   **Year 3291.**

And **Jotham** reigned sixteen years.   2 Kings 15: 33.

In year seventeen years of Pekah reigned Ahaz. 2 Kings 16:1.

1 Jotham being 3276, his year 16 is 3291. And as this year is reckoned to him, it is not his son's year 1, but only that of his accession.

For the 20 Jotham being spoken of when his reign is uniformly given as 16, see Part I, §§ 88—89.

1 Ahaz. Year 3292.

See the year preceding, which was only of the accession of Ahaz; and as that was his father's last; this next year is his own 1.

4 Ahaz (20 Jotham).   **Pekah's 20 end.** Year 3292.

.And Hosea Elah's son conspired a conspiracy against Pekah Remaliah's son (and smote him, and slew him, and reigned in his stead), in the year twenty of Jotham.   2 Kings 15: 30.

In year fifty and two years of Azariah Pekah reigned over Israel, twenty years.   2 Kings 15: 27.

As Jotham reigned only 16 years (see year 3291), his year 20 is year 4 of his successor.

52 Azariah is 3275, and 20 is 3295. See also the next year.

12 Ahaz.   Hosea's conspiracy. Year 3303.

.In year twelve of Ahaz king of Judah, Hosea, son of Elah, reigned over Israel, nine years.

Under years 3311 and 3313, which see, it is shown that they are respectively years 4 and 6 of Hezekiah. Year 1 of Hosea's actual reign is thus 3305. 2 Kings 15: 30, which places his reign apparently already two years earlier, in 3303, can therefore only mean this: Hosea conspired in 3303, and the words **and he smote him and slew him, and reigned in his stead,** being parenthetical, tell of events 2 years later.

Chronologers have been much troubled over what seemed to be confusion in Hosea's dates. But not a few Biblical seeming confusions are readily removed by just a parenthesis.

14 Ahaz.   1 Hosea. Year 3305.

.See next date, 16 Ahaz, which is expressly named as 3 Hosea. 3307, or 3

Hosea, less 2, is 3305, or 1 Hosea.

16 Ahaz.   3 Hosea.   Hezekiah accession.   **Year 3307.**

.Ahaz reigned sixteen years.   2 Kings 16: 2.

And it was in the year three of Hosea, king of Israel **that** Hezekiah reigned over Judah.   2 Kings 18: 1.

1 Ahaz being 3292, his year 16 is 3307.

The last year of his father being 3307, his own year 1 is 3308. But 4 and 6 Hezekiah are 7 and 9 Hosea, as is shown presently below. 1 Hezekiah is thus 4 Hosea, not 3. In 3 Hosea therefore only Hezekiah's accession took place.

His father died in 3 Hosea, which is duly reckoned as his, though Hezekiah had already begun is reign therein.

1 Hezekiah.   4 Hosea.   **Year 3308.**

.See the year preceding, 3307, which is the lat of Ahaz. This year is thus year 1 of his successor.

4 Hezekiah.   7 Hosea.   **Year 3311.**

.And the king of Assyria went up through the whole land, and went up to Samaria, and besieged it three years. In Hosea's ninth year he took Samaria. 2 Kings 17: 5—6.

And it was in the fourth year of king Hezekiah (the same is the seventh year of Hosea, son of Elah, king of Israel), Shalmanezer came up against Samaria, and besieged it. And at **the** end of three years they took it, in Hezekiah's year six, the same is Hosea's year nine.   2 Kings 18: 9—10.

1 Hezekiah is 3308, his year 4 is thus 3311.

These two data illustrate the utmost accuracy of Holy Writ, and the utmost need of the strictest adherence to its meaning. If Samaria was taken in 6 Hezekiah, or 9 Hosea after a siege of 3 years, then the siege began in 3 Hezekiah, or 6 Hosea. But 2 Kings 18: 9 takes special care to warn that the siege lasted only two years, and the 3 years are only current: since from 4 Hezekiah to 6 Hezekiah is only two years.

But if only two, how comes the text to speak of, as even the Revisers have it, **the end of** three years. Unless the dictionary is discarded this phrase can by no stretch of exegesis be made to mean aught less than three full years. In the versions, therefore, the text here presents an insurmountable difficulty.

And a wholly—needless one. For the text does not say **end**, but **ends**. And this Plural is not a Hebrew idiom for the Singular. The Singular is duly used in its proper place. The Plural here means its literal sense, more than one end.

When the Hebrew says, End of the year, it means the last day, week. or month of the year contemplated; say, December, or thereabout. But when it says, At the end of years, it contemplates two years, each with its own end. When two strings are tied together, its two ends make the tie. But it is the **upper** end of the one that is tied to the **lower** end of the other. And precisely so with the ends of years. Events covering, say, December and January may in the Hebrew be properly said to occur at the [two] ends of the years. At the ends of three years, may therefore be properly understood to mean that the siege lasted two years. But Samaria was taken at the **upper end** of the third year, say in Nisan or Tishri, as the case may be. Heb. 9: 26 is parallel here and a commentary: Now once at the consummation of the ages hath He been manifested to put away sin. At the end of one age, and at the beginning of another.

6 Hezekiah.   9 Hosea.   Year 3313.

See the discussion under the preceding year. His year 1 is 3308; his year 6 is thus 3313.

14 Hezekiah.   Year 3321.

And in year fourteen of king Hezekiah came up Senecherib against all the fenced cities of Judah, and took them.

2 Kings 18: 13.

His year 1 is 3308, and 14 is thus 3321.

Manasseh born.   Year 3325.

Manasseh was a son of twelve years at his reign.

2 Kings 21: 1.

Manasseh's year 1 is 3337, which see; less 12 is 3325.

29 Hezekiah, dies. **Year 3336.**

.And twenty and nine years **Hezekiah** reigned in Jerusalem.

2 Kings 18: 2

1 Hezekiah is 3308, his year 29 is thus 3336.

1 Manasseh. **Year 3337.**

And Hezekiah slept with his fathers, and Manasseh reigned in his stead. 2 Kings 20: 21.

3336 being Hezekiah's last year, the next, 3337, is year 1 of his successor.

Amon born. **Year 3370.**

A son of twenty and two years was Amon at his reign.

2 Kings 21: 19.

1 Amon is 3392, which see; less 22 is 3370.

Josiah born. **Year 3386.**

A son of eight years was Josiah at his reign.   2 Kings 22: 1.

1 Josiah is 3394, which see; less 8 is 3386.

55 Manasseh, dies. **Year 3391.**

And Manasseh reigned fifty and five years in Jerusalem.

2 Kings 21: 1.

His year 1 being 3337, his year 55 is 3391.

1 Amon. **Year 3392.**

And Manasseh slept with his fathers, and Amon his son reigned in his stead.   2 Kings 21: 18.

Manasseh's last year is 3391, and 3392 is thus his successor's year 1.

2 Amon, dies. **Year 3393.**

Amon reigned two years.   2 Kings 21: 19.

1 Amon being 3392, his year 2 is 3393.

1 Josiah.   Year 3394.

And the servants of Amon conspired against him, and put the king to death. And Josiah his son reigned in his stead.

2 Kings 21: 23, 26.

Amon's last year is 3393; the next, 3394 is thus year 1 of his successor.

Jehoiakim born.   Year 3400.

A son of twenty and five years was Jehoiakim at his reigning.

2 Kings 23: 36.

1 Jehoiakim is 3425, which see; less 25 is 3400.

8 Josiah.   Year 3401.

And in year eight of his reign **Josiah** began to seek after the God of David.   2 Chron. 34: 3.

1 Josiah being 3394, his year 8 is 3401.

Jehoahaz born.   Year 3402.

Joahaz was a son of three and twenty years at his reign.

2 Chron. 36: 2.

Jehoahaz reigned in 3425, which see; less 23 is 3402.

12 Josiah.   Year 3405.

And in year 12 **Josiah** began to purge Judah and Jerusalem from the high places.   2 Chron 34: 3.

13 Josiah.   Year 3406.

Jeremiah, to whom the word of the Lord **came** in year thirteen of Josiah's reign.   Jer. 1: 2.

From year thirteen of Josiah, the word of the Lord was unto me. Jer. 25: 3.

18 Josiah.   **Year 3411.**

And it was in year eighteen of Josiah that the king sent Shaphan the scribe to the house of the Lord.   2 Kings 22: 3.

No such passover had been kept from the days of the Judges, but in year eighteen of king Josiah was this passover kept.

2 Kings 23:22.

Zedekiah born.   **Year 3415.**

Zedekiah was a son of twenty and one years at his reigning.

2 Kings 24: 18.

1 Zedekiah is 3236, less 21 is 3415.

Jehoiachin born.   **Year 3418.**

Jehoiachin was a son of eighteen years at his reigning.

2 Kings 24: 8.

Jehoiachin was a son of eight years at his reigning.

2 Chron. 36: 9.

Jehoichin's reign was in 3436, less 18 is 3418.

The difference of age here, 8 and 18, is discussed in Part I, §§ 21—23. If 8 in Chronicles be not a copyist's error, he was 8 years only 3425. For if in 3426, that year would have to be added to the List, and Numerics testify against this, as shown in Part III.

31 Josiah, dies.   **Year 3424.**

Josidah reigned thirty and one years.   2 Kings 22: 1.

1 Josiah being 3394, his year 31 is 3424.

1 Jehoahaz.   **1 Jehoiakim.**   **Year 3425.**

Pharaoh Necho slew Josiah, and the people of the land took Jehoahaz, and made him king in his father's stead.

2 Kings 23: 29—30.

Jehoahaz reigned three months. And Pharaoh Necho made Eliakim, son of Josiah, king, and changed his name to Jehoiakim. 2 Kings 23: 31, 34.

3 Jehoiakim.   Year 3427.

In year three of Jehoiakim Nebuchadnezzar went to Jerusalem. Dan. 1: 1.

1 Jehoiakim being 3425, his year 3 is 3427.

4 Jehoiakim.   1 Nebuchadnezzar.   Year 3428.

The word which was unto Jeremiah in the fourth year of Jehoiakim, the same is in the first year of Nebuchadnezzar.

Jer. 25: 1.

From year thirteen of Josiah and unto this day, these three and twenty years.   Jer 25: 3.

1 Jehoiakim being 3425, his year 4 is 3428.

13 Josiah is 3406. It being year 1 of the era reckoned from it, its year 23 is also 3428.

5 Jehoiakim.   2 Nebuchadnezzar.   Year 3429.

And it was in the fifth year of Jehoiakim that they proclaimed a fast. Jer. 36: 9.

And in year two of Nebuchadnezzar's reign Nebuchadnezzar dreamed dreams.   Dan. 2: 1.

3425 being 1 Jehoiakim, his year 5 is 3429.

6 Jehoiakim.   Year 3430.

In year three of Jehoiakim's reign Nebuchadnezzar spake unto the master of his eunuchs that he should bring in of Israel's sons, of the seed royal, and they should be nourished three years.

Dan 1: 1, 3, 5.

3 Jehoiakim is 3427, and 3 is 3430.

7 Nebuchadnezzar.   Year 3434.

This is the people who Nebuchadnezzar carried away captive: in the seventh year three thousand Jews. Jer. 52: 28.

1 Nebuchadnezzar being 3428, 7 is 3434.

That this is the seventh year of Nebuchadnezzar is clear from the next sentence of the verse, which goes on with the words, in the year eighteen of Nebuchadnezzar.

11 Jehoiakim. **Year 3435.**

Jehoiakim reigned eleven years in Jerusalem. 2 Kings 23: 36.

1 Jehoiakim being 3425, his year 11 is 3435.

1 Jehoiachin.   1 Zedekiah. **Year 3426.**

Jehoiachin reigned three months. And the Babylon king made Mattaniah king in his stead, and changed his name to Zedekiah.

2 Kings 24: 8, 17.

4 Zedekiah. **Year 3439.**

Seraiah went with Zedekiah to Babylon in the fourth year of his reign. Jer. 51: 59.

1 Zedekiah being 3436, his year 4 is 3439.

5 Zedekiah. **Year 3440.**

On day five of the month (the same is the fifth year of king Jehoiakin's captivity), the word of the Lord surely was unto Ezekiel. Ezek. 1: 2.

Jehoiachin was taken to Babylon after a reign of only 3 months, in 3436, his year 1; his year 5 is thus 3440 and 5 Zedekiah.

Year 1 of this captivity being 3436, its year 27 is 3462.

37 Captivity Jehoiachin.   1 Evil Merodach. **Year 3472.**

And it was in year thirty and seven years of Jehoiachin's captivity that Evil Merodach, in the year of his reign, lifted up Jehoiachin's head, and brought him forth out of prison.

Jer. 52: 31.

Year 1 of this Captivity being 3436, its year 37 is 3472.

1 Darius. 69 Captivity. Belshazzar dies. Year 3515.

In that night Belshazzar the Chaldean king was slain, and Darius the Mede received the kingdom.   Dan. 5: 30—31.

In year 1 of Darius of the seed of the Medes I Daniel understood by the books the number of years.   Dan 9: 1—2.

See also the next year.

2 Darius. 70 Captivity ends. Year 3516.

In the eighth month, in year two of Darius, the word of the Lord was unto Zechariah.   Zech 1: 1.

And the angel of the Lord answered and said: O Lord of hosts, how long wilt Thou not have mercy on Jerusalem and on the cities of Judah against which Thou hast had indignation these seventy years? Zech. 1: 12.

This and the verses following fix the time of the angel's question in year 70 of the Captivity. The promise, I am jealous for Jerusalem and for Zion with a great jealousy, I am sore displeased with the nations that are at ease, therefore I am returned to Jerusalem with mercies (verses 14—16), could not be spoken after the decree of Cyrus for the Restoration. With this agrees also the call unto repentance in verse 3, Return unto Me, saith the Lord of hosts, and I will return unto you. What Daniel was led to do in his Chapter 9 without a message individually, God's people are here called on to do through a special messenger also nationally.

This Darius is therefore not Hystaspes, but the Mede of Daniel. 2 Darius the Mede is thus year 70 of the Captivity, or 3516, and 1 Darius is 3515. And as the 70 years of Captivity are followed by the 483 years of Daniel's 70 weeks which begin with the Decree of 1 Cyrus, it is clearly the purpose of Scripture to assign to this Darius only to only two years chronologically, whatever the length of his reign, sole or joint with Cyrus.

But because of Hag. 1:1, "In year two of Darius the king came the word of the Lord by Haggai unto Zerubbabel, governor of Judah," which Darius is here clearly other than the Mede, since a governor of Judah is already there, the commentators have uniformly taken the two Dariuses as one. But the language in Zechariah forbids their identification. The angels question as to the end of the **desolation** is dated day twenty-four, month eleven. The last message of Hag. (2: 20) to Zerubbabel is exactly two months **earlier**, both being in 2 Darius. This rules out the identification of the one Darius with the other.

There remains, however, this difficulty: In Zech. 7: 1—5 it is, And it was in year four of king Darius that they of Bethel sent men, saying, Should I weep in the fifth month, as I have done these many years? This inquiry is about continuing to fast in memory of the burning of the Jerusalem Temple which took place in the fifth month. And the Lord's answer is in the Revised Version, When ye fasted in the fifth month, even these seventy years, did ye at all fast unto Me? This rendering makes the 70 years end in both 2 Darius and 4 Darius. But Holy writ, in the original, presents no such confusion. Instead of **even these** the Hebrew says **and this**, thus entirely changing the character of the sentence into a parenthesis, When ye fasted (and this moreover seventy years), did ye at all fast unto Me?

As this inquiry, however, was clearly sent at least 2 years after 2 Darius the Mede, there are here two possibilities: (1) The Mede may have reigned at least 4 years, of which only two are assigned to him; the rest of his reign, being concurrent with that of Cyrus, being assigned to Cyrus. (2) Zechariah prophesied in the days of two Dariuses: the Mede of Daniel, and the Darius of Haggai. The second explanation is favoured by the following consideration.

Haggai speaks of Darius **the king**, when he first mentions him, in 1: 1. Having thus identified him, he can afford to omit the title when mentioning him again (only once) in 2: 10. Zechariah, however, omits the title when he speaks of the Mede, both in 1: 1 and 7. But in 7: 1 he adds the title. If the two are different kings in Zechariah, this distinction may be to indicate this expressly. Now the first three times the Mede is mentioned by Daniel, a certain peculiarity attaches to its manner. In Dan. 5: 31—6: 1 it is, And Darius the Mede received the kingdom. It pleased Darius to set over the kingdom an hundred and twenty-seven satraps. In Dan. 9: 1 it is, In year one of Darius, son of Ahasuerus, of the seed of the Medes, who was made king over the realm of the Chaldeans.

Not took the kingdom, but received it. And he was **made** king. Daniel elsewhere does call Darius king, but his reluctance therewith where least expected, together with his peculiar phrasing here, strongly suggest that the

Mede was only a subordinate king. And this would also explain the distinction made by Zechariah, which otherwise might seem needless. Darius the king was apparently not so much a king as a vice-king, a fact indicated by Daniel, and studiously held to by Zechariah.

1 Cyrus.   490 years begin.   **Year 3517.**

And in year 1 of Cyrus the king of Persia the Lord stirred up Cyrus king of Persia, and he made a proclamation, throughout all his kingdom, saying: the Lord hath charged me to build Him a house in Jerusalem. Whosoever there is among you of all his people, let him go up. Ezra 1: 1—3.

See Part 1, § § 52—58 for an extended discussion of the beginning of these 490 years.

2 Cyrus.   **Year 3518.**

And in the second year of their coming unto the house of God in Jerusalem began Zerubbabel and the rest of the brethren to set forward the work of the house of the Lord.   Ezra 3: 8.

And when the seventh month was come, the people gathered as one man to Jerusalem.   Ezra 3: 1.

As year 1 of their coming was 1 Cyrus, year 2 thereof is 2 Cyrus.

3 Cyrus.   **Year 3519.**

In year three of Cyrus, king of Persia, a thing was revealed to Daniel. Dan. 10: 1.

1 Cyrus being 3517, his year 3 is 3519.

49 Years end.   **Year 3565.**

Seventy weeks are cut off for thy people. From the going forth of the word to restore Jerusalem unto an anointed one, a prince, shall be seven sevens and sixty and two sevens.

Dan 9: 24—25.

Year 1 of the 490 years being 3517, year 49 is 3565.

It is agreed by all that the **sevens** here or weeks (heptads is better) mean years, as the only meaning possible to give sense. Accordingly, "years" is omitted without risk to the understanding of the meaning. The other time terms, day and month, are oft omitted as self-understood from the context. See under year 3145 for a similar omission of **year** for perhaps the same reason.

Anna's husband dies. Year 3916.

There was one Anna a prophetess, she was advanced in many days, having lived with a husband seven years from her virginity, and she had been a widow even for eighty four years.

Luke 2: 36—37.

The presence of Anna in the Temple was when the Lord was some five weeks old, in 3999, which see; less 84 is 3916.

If the sense of the phrase, Having lived with a husband seven years from her virginity could be fixed to the meaning that her married life lasted only seven years, at the end of which the husband died, the year 3909 (which is seven years back from 3916) would have to be added to the List. But other interpretations are possible, and Numerics also make against the insertion of that year in the List.

Annunciation by Gabriel. Year 3998.

Now it came to pass while Zacharias executed the priest's office before God the Lord's angel appeared to him and said, I am Gabriel. And after these days Elizabeth his wife conceived, and she hid herself five months. And in the sixth month the angel Gabriel was sent from God unto Mary. Luke 1: 8—27.

This was a year before 3999; less 1 is 3998.

The Lord was born in 3999, which see. The angel appeared to Mary at least nine months before the Birth. But he appeared to Zacharias six months before appearing to Mary. The first Annunciation by Gabriel was therefore at least fifteen months before the birth of the Holy Child. The narrative does not permit the extension of these fifteen months into 24, so as to throw back the first Annunciation two years instead of one.

Birth of the Lord. Year 3999.

The 483 years, or the sixty nine weeks, of Daniel from the Commandment to the Messiah Prince began in 3517, which is their year 1. Their year 483 is thus 3999.

See Part I, § § 52—67 for the discussion as to the end of the 483 years.

The Lord 12 years old.   **Year 4011.**

And His [the Lord's] parents went yearly to Jerusalem, and when he was twelve years old they went up after the custom of the feast. Luke 2: 41—42.

The Lord was born in 3999, and 12 is 4011.

1 Tiberius.   **Year 4015.**

15 Tiberius is 4029, which see. 1 Tiberius is thus 14 years back, or 4015

The question whether the years of Tiberius are reckoned here from his sole reign, or from his joint reign with Augustus, belongs to another department of investigation. What we are here concerned with is only the year which the **Bible** calls the fifteenth of Tiberius.

15 Tiberius. The Lord 30. Year 1 of ministry.   **Year 4029**

Now in the fifteenth year of the reign of Tiberius Caesar the word of God came unto John. And he came preaching a baptism of repentance. Now it came to pass when all the people were baptized Jesus also having been baptized, the Holy Spirit descended upon him. And Jesus Himself, when He began, was about thirty years of age.   Luke 3: 1—23.

The Lord was born in 3999, and 30 is 4029.

The Holy Spirit descended upon the Lord at his baptism, and it was then declared by the voice from heaven, This is My Son the beloved in whom I am well-pleased. Immediately thereafter the Spirit driveth Him into the wilderness for forty days. The ministry thus began not later than some six weeks after the baptism. John was baptizing in 15 Tiberius. Considering that it was the word of God that came to John, that the Lord Himself acknowledged His baptism as from Heaven, and that He described His own baptism as fulfilling all righteousness, it is not permissible to suppose that the Lord in any wise delayed his baptism, least of all so as to move it beyond the one year so minutely marked by the various notes of time attached thereto. 15 Tiberius, therefore, as it was the year of the Baptism was thus also the first year of the Ministry.

Year 2 of ministry.   **Year 4030.**

And the passover was nigh, and Jesus went up to Jerusalem. When He was at the passover many believed on him.

John 2: 13—23.

This follows the statement in verse eleven that, This was the beginning of His signs. All that precedes, therefore, in chapter 1—2 thus took place in the year which ended two weeks before this passover. The narrative does not permit the events of these two chapters to be crowded into the two weeks before the passover. This passover, therefore, is in the year which follows that of the baptism, or 4030.

Year 3 of ministry.   **Year 4031.**

After these things was a feast of the Jews.
Now the Passover, the feast of the Jews, was nigh.

John 5: 1 ; 6: 4.

As between the Passover of 4030 in chapter II and this Passover of chapter VI the feast of chapter VI intervened, the two are distinct Passovers. And as only one Passover was kept in the year, if the first was in 4030, the second was in 4031. On the other hand, the narrative in none of the four Gospels warrants the **necessity** that the interval between chapters II and VI covered more than one Passover.

The Gospels of Matthew, Mark, and Luke, attest themselves as written before the destruction of Jerusalem, since each reports the Lord's prophecy thereof, without the comment that it was already fulfilled at the time of their writing. Luke expressly does this with the famine foretold by Agabus in Acts II: 28 by adding, Which came to pass in the days of Claudius.

Of the Gospel of John there is no reason to doubt the uniform tradition that it was written late in the nineties of the first century. It thus found its way in the Universal Church, specially amidst the persecutions of those days, slowly and late. Now it is from John's Gospel alone that we learn that the ministry of the Lord was more than one year, since he names three Passovers. The three Synoptics leave one with the impression, though not necessarily, that the Ministry covered only one year. Some of the early Church Fathers accordingly held to a ministry of one year. The early fixed impression of a short ministry was too strong to become readily replaced by a careful noting of the much later notes of time in John. All error, however, soon betrays itself by inconsistency. Accordingly confusion about the time of the Ministry came early and spread wide. Even the years of the Roman Consuls, about which ordinarily there surely need be no difficulty, are here confused: some of the Fathers assigning the year of the Passion to one set of Consuls, others to another. In time, however, specially after a better acquaintance with John, the misapprehension passed away, and the longer Ministry has been in possession of the field for some 16 centuries until attacked again by the scholarly Henry Browne in his Ordo Saeculorum (who had, however, a theory to defend: a fact which always works havoc with even well meaning folk of Browne's calibre). The equally able and scholarly Jarvis, however, in his Chronological Introduction **assumes** four Passovers, because **a** feast PERHAPS stands for **the** feast; and this in turn **probably** is a Passover.

Thus the case had been standing until Daniel began to be studied in earnest, when once the Church could breathe more freely. Then it was found that Daniel says in 9: 27, And he shall make a covenant with many for one week, and in the midst of the week [or for half of the week] he shall cause the sacrifice of the oblation to cease. This was at once applied to the Lord Jesus: that His ministry was to be half of a week of years, or three years and half. This verse of Daniel is **the only authority in or out of the Bible** for a ministry longer than the three current years assigned it by John.

Now Daniel's "he" **may** indeed refer to the Lord, but **may** is only a possibility. To be transformed into **does**, it must first be demonstrated as a fact, and this demonstration has not even. been attempted.

Now John is clear three Passovers only, and the utmost length of the ministry not a fortnight over three years. And even thus it must begin **exactly** on Nisan 1 of 4029, since the Passion was on Nisan 14, 4032. Daniel is not only not so clear, he is designedly obscure, since unfulfilled Prophecy is to be understood only by the wise, the spiritual. If so plain that the sons of darkness also could understand it, its fulfillment might be hindered by their master. And the clear must never be allowed to be darkened by the obscure.

The language of Gabriel to Daniel is: Dan. 9: 26—27, The Anointed one shall be cut off, and the people of the prince to come shall destroy the city. and his [or its] end shall be with a flood, and even unto the end shall be war; desolations are determined. And he shall make a firm covenant with many for a week, and for the half of the week he shall cause the sacrifice and the oblation to cease, and upon the wing of abominations is one that maketh desolate: and even unto the consummation, and what is determined shall be poured out upon the desolate (or desolator).

120

The original having no punctuation marks, perhaps even no spaces between the words, the reader need not be bound by the interpretation as given here in the punctuation. But some things are clear here, in spite of the confessed obscurity of this passage:

(1) the Anointed one of verse 26 is clearly the Christ, our Blessed (and precious) Lord Jesus. (2) The coming Prince, whose people shall destroy the City and the Holy place is (a) not the Lord, since the City is destroyed not so much by the prince himself as by the people. If this prince is Lord, his people are either the Jews or Christians. Jerusalem was destroyed by the— Romans. Moreover, the end of the Lord was not with a Flood (if the meaning is **His**), neither literal nor figurative, there was no war at the time of the Cross. Again, the Cross was not the end of the One who hath no end. (b) not Titus, nor Vespasian, since both were Roman emperors, princes, and both had their part in the destruction of the City. The prophecy specifies one prince, not princes. Neither Titus nor Vespasian was emperor, or prince at the beginning of the war in Judaea, and Titus was not prince even at its end. Nero, Otho, and Vitellius were the Roman emperors in the same year with Vespasian. If by the people of the of the coming prince Rome is meant, Prince cannot here be any one emperor, as long as officially as many five can be reckoned up under whom the destruction of the City took place. (c) not Antiochus Epiphanes, who is king of only one of the four kingdoms into which Alexander's Greek Empire was divided. A people of the Coming Prince requires homogeneity. Assyria, Babylon, Medo-Persia, Alexander's Greece, could each be spoken of truly as the people of a Prince. But after Alexander the four kingdoms were not only separate, they were not all even Greek, Egypt being one of the four. Moreover, it was the people that was to do the destroying, not the Prince. The then status of both Vespasian and Titus justifies Gabriel's words if applied to Rome, but not to Antiochus.

Now, whoever this Coming Prince be, a person or a kingdom (in Daniel specially king is at times used for kingdom), is here bulkily interposed between the Messiah and the Covenanter. That this Covenanter is the Lord after the long, not even parenthetical, interruption (read here the verses again, please), is of course not absolutely impossible, since in more than one sense is the word of the Lord true that, All things are possible to him that believeth. But whoever insists that this Covenanter **must** be the Lord, raises his own opinion to the rank of evidence.

And with the Lord as a mere possibility as Daniel's Covenanter, and not as a demonstrated certainty, the whole scheme of a ministry of 3 years and a half, with its chronology and prophecies—collapses. No true Science can permit mere possibilities for its basis, least of all Bible Chronology. Such liberty, so justly condemned in every species of Unbelief, is the very last to be taken by those professing to stand and contend for the Faith which needs no **such** armour.

As John mentions only three Passovers, the attempt was early made to supply a fourth. to bring the Gospel narrative into harmony, with the longer ministry supposedly required from Daniel. John 5: 1 readily lends itself thereto. After these things was a feast of the Jews, **a** feast, not the feast. Some manuscripts have **the**, which is rejected by Westcott and Hort without even an alternative and by the Revisers, though with a note about the other reading. Numerics are so far with Westcott and Hort. The insertion of the definite article here would make this feast as a Passover more probable, but no more than probable. John's mention of only three Passovers is clear, his abstaining from naming a fourth, when having the opportunity to do so, is equally clear. This fourth Passover is thus only a remote possibility. With these **facts** before us the three years and a **half** ministry, with the Daniel interpretation based on it, and the prophetic scheme it involves, is relegated to the domain of mere pious—guesswork, as against established facts required for any scientific Bible Chronology or Interpretation.

The Cross and Resurrection.   Year 4032.

Now it was the Preparation of the Passover. Saith Pilate to them, Shall I crucify your king? Then he delivered Him to them to be crucified. John 19: 14—16.

On the first **day** of the week they came to the tomb, and two men stood by them in dazzling apparel, and said unto them, He is not here, He is risen. He spake to you saying, He must be crucified, and the third day rise again. And lo, two of them were going that very day to Emmaus, and Jesus Himself drew near and went with them. But their eyes were holden that they should not know Him. And they said to Him the things concerning Jesus, how the chief priests and rulers crucified Him. It is not the third day since all these things came to pass.   Luke 24: 1—21.

The apostles, to whom He presented Himself alive after His passion for forty days. And as they were looking, He was taken up, and a cloud received Him out of their sight.   Acts 1: 3—9.

The Cross was at the Passover, two wees already in the New Year 4032.

The Resurrection was two days after the Cross, and the Ascension was forty days ofter the Resurrection. All this in the one year 4032.

As the Lord rose on the first day of the week, or Sunday, it is the third day from Friday. The Lord Himself says in Matt. 16: 21 that He must be killed, and be raised the **third day**. In Luke 9: 22 it is again, The Son of Man must be killed, and the third day be raised up. The two angels at the Tomb repeated this same third day to the women. The Emmaus disciples tell the Lord Himself that this Sunday is the third day from the Cross. In 1 Cor. 15: 4 Paul also says, He hath been raised on the third day. Against these five times naming the third day stands Mark 9: 31 with its, The Son of Man must be killed, and after three days rise. As this passage of Mark is only the parallel to Matthew and Luke, it is explained by them, not they darkened by it. Namely: that the phrase After three days may mean three current as well as full days, so that the phrase may cover only two nights. The statement of the Lord that the Son of Man must be in the heart of the earth three days and nights, has bearing here until the metaphor Heart of the earth is cleared of its obscurity. A tomb on the surface of the ground clearly even less the heart of the earth than a grave only six feet beneath the sod. The recent notion of a Thursday Cross (Dr. Torrey being even content with nothing short of a Wednesday for it), in order to give three nights in the tomb, must therefore be rejected as an erroneous attempt to explain a hard saying of the Lord with the same impatience that has been the intellectual, if not also the spiritual undoing of the Higher Critics.

For the settlement of the exact year of the Cross, involving also the length of the Ministry, the testimony of the moon is needful, since the Cross being on 14 Nisan came on the day of about the full moon. Now the moon, having no theological predilections, does not readily lend itself to a one year ministry, refusing to be full on the required Friday. The One year ministry advocates are thus driven to a Thursday Cross, with the moon more tractable for the year of their choice. It is thus that Error ever proves itself, by its inability to stand alone, it ever requiring others to follow in its train. Accordingly, those who favour the Cross on Thursday are generally found only among the upholders of the Shorter Ministry. In his Introduction to the Gospels, an earlier work, the comparatively young Westcott, impressed by Browne's ability and learning, did raise the question whether Thursday might not after all be the day. But he did not commit himself thereto. But he had already committed himself to the dynamical theory of the Inspiration of Scripture (whatever that means), as opposed to the mechanical [verbal] held by the present writer, in a special chapter thereon. This distinction (stated by him shortly before his death in a letter to the writer), not found in the Bible, but invented to enable one to hold citizenship in two warring states at the same time, Orthodoxy and Rationalism, left even the great Westcott open to grave error, with the possibility to him of the Crucifixion occurring on a Thursday as the fruit thereof. But of all the scholars worth while known to the writer Westcott was the only one who at all came even that near to the Thursday Cross, outside the short ministry advocates.

But there is also Luke 23: 54, And it was the day of Preparation, and the Sabbath began to dawn. To a scholar of the rank of Westcott the possibility that Preparation unqualified can mean aught else than the regular Friday might have been very remote indeed; all the more so when John in 19: 14 takes special pains to add "of the Passover" after "Preparation" to show that just as that Sabbath was a double sabbath, what he calls a high day, so that Friday was a double Preparation of Sabbath and Passover.

As to the Wednesday Cross, the utmost that is required by the hard saying of the Lord is **three** nights in the heart of the earth. But this gives Him—four, or the Lord rose on—Saturday. Verily, even just a little arithmetic doth save from very much blundering. **He that hath wisdom let him** COUNT.

TABLE I.

Beyond 4032 the Bible offers no data for fixing any one year or period of years.

The 245 individual years which alone are obtainable from the Bible are herewith presented in tabular form for ready inspection and quick reference. The first column at the of the page gives the years from Adam. They are designated the heading A.M. as Years of the World (anno mundi) solely in deference to usage, since Adam's year begins on Saturday, if not indeed on Friday, while the astronomical year clearly begins with a Wednesday. The actual age of the universe, while it clearly begins in the first verse of Genesis, does not necessarily begin with the Sunday of verse Between verses 1 and 3 much may have taken place, and in verse 2 much actually does take place before the evening, which with its morning makes up the first day. Anno Mundi is thus not strictly accurate for the years of Bible Chronology, which can be reckoned only from the creation of Adam.

The second column gives these same years in terms of B.C. (before Christ). The year of the Lord's birth, 3999 from Adam is demonstrably 4 B.C., four years before Year 1 of the Christian Era. 3999 and 4 thus give 4003 as the year before which Adam can be said to be one year old. He is 1 year old in 4002, and the sum of the two reckonings is 4003. He is 2 years old in 4001, and 130 in 3873, the sum of the two always being 4003. For the years after B.C., the years A.D. (anno domini), the years of the Christian era, 3999 being 4002 is 1 B.C., and the next year 1 A.D., is 4003. The difference between the years A.M. and A.D. is always 4002. Thus the present year 1922 is 5924 from Adam, and their difference 4002, The sum 4003 for B.C. years, the difference 4002 for A.D. years ever holds in the relation of the two of the two reckonings.

Birth years are marked with (^{1}) before the year, death with (^{2}). The year of Enoch's Translation, being of exit, but not of his death, is marked (*).

Of the Judges raised up for delivering Israel it is expressly that after the death of the judge Israel sinned again. The presumption is, therefore, that at the end of the 40 connected with her name Deborah died. But though judged Israel then, it was Barak upon whom she called deliver. As Barak was no judge, neither fails strictly the category of Judg. 2: 18—19. Accordingly, the year 2770 is only questioned as a death year.

The age at one's death is often distinctly stated, in others it only inferred. This distinction is observed thus in the Terah 205, dies (see year 2083) means that his age at is specially stated, as distinct from the case of his back to Shem. On the other hand, Shem dies, 600 (see year 2158) means that his age at death is not though readily ascertainable otherwise.

PERIOD 1. ADAM TO THE FLOOD.

		A.M.	B.C.
	Adam Created	0	4003
1	Adam 130, Seth born	^{1}130	3873
2	Seth 105, Enosh born	^{1}235	3768
3	Enosh 90, Kenan born	^{1}325	3678
4	Kenan 70, Mahalaleel	^{1}395	3608
5	Mahalaleel 65, Jared born	^{1}460	3543
6	Jared 162, Enoch born	^{1}622	3381
7	Enoch 65, Methuselah born	^{1}687	3316

		A.M.	B.C.
8	Methuselah 187, Lamech born	¹874	3129
9	Adam 930, dies	²930	3073
10	Enoch 365, translated	*987	3016
11	Seth 912, dies	1042	2961
12	Lamech 182, Noah born	¹1056	2947
13	Enosh 905, dies	²1140	2863
14	Kenan 910, dies	²1235	2768
15	Mahalaleel 895, dies	²1290	2713
16	Jared 962, dies	²1422	2581
17	Flood decreed	1536	2467
18	Noah 500, Japhet born	¹1556	2447
19	Shem born	¹1558	2445
20	Lamech 777, dies	²1651	2352
21	Methuselah 969, dies. Noah 600. The Flood.	²1656	2347
	13 x 13 x 41 x 3	20,787	

PERIOD 2. FLOOD TO COVENANT

		A.M.	B.C.
22	Noah 601, Flood subsides	1547	2346
23	Shem 100, Arphaxad born	¹1658	2345
24	Arphaxad 35, Shelah born	¹1693	2310
25	Shelah 30, Eber born	¹1723	2280
26	Eber 34, Peleg born	¹1757	2246
27	Peleg 30, Reu born	¹1787	2216
28	Reu 32, Serug born	¹1519	2184
29	Serug 30, Nahor born	¹1849	2154
30	Nahor 29, Terah born	¹1878	2125
31	Terah 70, Haran born	¹1948	2055
32	Peleg dies, age 239	²1996	2007
33	Nahor dies, age 148	²1997	2006
34	Noah, 950, dies	²2006	1997
35	Abraham born	¹2008	1995
36	Sarah born	¹2017	1986
37	Reu dies, age 239	²2026	1977
38	Serug dies, age 230	²2049	1954

		A.M.	B.C.
39	Terah, 205, dies	²2083	1920
40	Abraham 86, Ishmael born	¹2094	1909
41	Arphaxad dies, age 438	²2096	1907
42	Abraham 90, the Covenant	2107	1896
	13 x 43 x 2 x 2 x 2 x 3 x 3	40,248	

Period 3. Covenant to Exodus.

		A.M.	B.C.
43	Abraham 100, Isaac born	¹2108	1895
44	Shelah dies, age 433	²2126	1977
45	Sarah, 127, dies	²2144	1859
46	Isaac 40, marries Rebecca	2148	1855
47	Shem dies, age 600	²2158	1845
48	Isaac 60, Esau and Jacob born	¹2168	1835
49	Abraham 175, dies	²2183	1820
50	Eber dies, age 464	2187	1816
51	Esau 40, marries Judith	2208	1795
52	Ishmael 137, dies	²2231	1772
53	Jacob with Laban, age 77	2245	1758
54	Jacob marries Leah and Rachel	2252	1751
55	Joseph born	¹2259	1744
56	Jacob's years of service end	2265	1738
57	Joseph, 17, sold into Egypt	2276	1727
58	Joseph in prison	2287	1716
59	Isaac 180, dies	²2288	1715
60	Joseph 30, is before Pharaoh	2289	1714
61	Seven years of plenty end	2296	1707
62	Year 1 of Famine	2297	1706
63	Year 2 of Famine, Jacob 130	2298	1705
64	Jacob 147, dies	²2315	1688
65	Joseph 110, dies	²2369	1634
66	Aaron born	¹2454	1549
67	Moses born	¹2457	1546
68	Moses 40	2497	1506
69	Caleb born	¹2498	1505

		A.M.	B.C.
70	The Exodus	2537	1466
	7 x 19 x 2 x 2 x 2 x 2 x 2 x 3 x 5	63,840	

Period 4. Exodus to Temple.

		A.M.	B.C.
71	Year 2 of Exodus, Caleb 40	2538	1465
72	Year 40 of Exodus	2576	1427
73	Year 1 in Canaan	2577	1426
74	Caleb 85, Division of Land	2583	1420
75	Elders die	²2610	1393
76	40 years and Oppressions begin	2611	1392
77	Cushan Oppression ends	2618	1385
78	40 Years end, Othniel dies	²2650	1353
79	80 Years begin, Oppression	2651	1352
80	Eglon's Oppression ends	2668	1335
81	80 Years end, Ehud dies	²2730	1273
82	40 Years begin, Oppression	2731	1272
83	Jabin's Oppression ends	2750	1253
84	40 Years end	2770	1233
85	40 Years begin, Oppression	2771	1232
86	Midian Oppression ends	2777	1226
87	40 Years end, Gideon dies	²2810	1193
88	1 Abimelech	2811	1192
89	3 Abimelech, dies	²2813	1190
90	1 Tola	2814	1189
91	Eli born	¹2830	1173
92	23 Tola, dies	²2836	1167
93	1 Jair	2837	1166
94	22 Jair, dies	²2858	1145
95	300 Years' Possession, and Ammon Oppression end	2876	1127
96	1 Jephthah	2877	1126
97	6 Jephthah, dies	²2882	1121
98	1 Ibzan	2883	1120
99	Eli High Priest and Judge	2887	1116
100	7 Ibzan, dies	²2889	1114

		A.M.	B.C.
101	1 Elon	2890	1113
102	10 Elon, dies	²2899	1104
103	1 Abdon	2900	1103
104	8 Abdon, dies	²2907	1096
105	Eli 98, dies	²2927	1076
106	Ishbosheth born	¹2935	1068
107	David born	¹2944	1059
108	Philistines 40 years end	2947	1056
109	Mephibosheth born	¹2969	1034
110	Samuel dies	²2971	1032
111	1 Saul	2972	1031
112	2 Saul, dies	²2973	1030
113	1 David, 1 Ishbosheth	2974	1029
114	2 Ishbosheth	2975	1028
115	7 David	2980	1023
116	40 David, dies; Rehoboam born	²¹3013	990
117	1 Solomon	3014	989
118	3 Solomon	3016	987
119	4 Solomon, Temple begun	3017	986
	(13 x 23 x 29 x 2 x 2 x 2 x 2) + 1	138,737	

Period 5. Temple to Captivity.

		A.M.	B.C.
120	11 Solomon, Temple finished	3024	979
121	24 Solomon, house finished	3037	966
122	40 Solomon, dies	²3053	950
123	1 Rehoboam, 1 Jeroboam	3054	949
124	3 Rehoboam	3056	947
125	5 Rehoboam	3058	945
126	17 Rehoboam, dies, age 58	²3070	933
127	1 Abijam, 18 Jeroboam	3071	932
128	3 Abijam, dies; 20 Jeroboam	²3073	930
129	1 Asa	3074	929
130	2 Asa; 22 Jeroboam, dies; 1 Nadab	²3075	928
131	3 Asa; 2 Nadab, dies; 1 Baasha	²3076	927

132	Jehoshaphat born	¹3080	923
133	10 Asa	3083	920
134	15 Asa	3088	915
135	26 Asa; 24 Baasha, dies; 1 Elah	²3099	904
136	27 Asa; 2 Elah, dies, 1 Omri	²3100	903
137	31 Asa, 5 Omri	3104	899
138	6 Omri in Tirzah	3105	898
139	35 Asa, Jehoram born	¹3108	895
140	38 Asa; 12 Omri, dies; Ahab Accession	²3111	892
141	39 Asa, 1 Ahab	3112	891
142	41 Asa, dies	²3114	889
143	1 Jehoshaphat, 4 Ahab	3115	888
144	3 Jehoshaphat	3117	886
145	Ahaziah born	¹3126	877
146	17 Jehoshaphat, 20 Ahab, 1 Ahaziah, joint	3131	872
147	18 Jehoshaphat, 1 Jehoram joint	3132	871
148	19 Jehoshaphat	3133	870
149	20 Jehoshaphat, 1 Ahaziah sole	3134	869
150	21 Jehoshaphat, 2 Ahaziah sole	3135	868
151	22 Jehoshaphat, 1 Jehoram sole, 5 Jehoram joint	3136	867
152	25 Jehoshaphat, dies, age 59; Jehoram Accession, 4 Jehoram Israel	²3139	864
153	1 Jehoram, 5 Jehoram Israel	3140	863
154	6 Jehoram, sick	3145	858
155	8 Jehoram, dies, Ahaziah's Accession	²3147	856
156	1 Ahaziah, dies, age 23; Jehoram Israel dies, Joash born	¹²3148	855
157	1 Attaliah, 1 Jehu	3149	854
158	6 Attaliah, dies	²3154	849
159	1 Joash, 7 Jehu	3155	848
160	Amaziah born	3170	833
161	28 Jehu, dies	²3176	827
162	23 Joash, 1 Jehoahaz	3177	826
163	37 Joash, 1 Joash Israel joint	3191	812
164	17 Jehoahaz, Zechariah dies	3193	810
165	40 Joash, dies, age 47; 1 Joash of Israel sole	3194	809
166	1 Amaziah; 2 Joash, of Israel	3195	808
167	1 Jeroboam joint	3198	805

168	14 Amaziah, Azariah born		¹3208	795
169	15 Amaziah; 16 Joash, dies; 1 Jeroboam sole		²3209	794
170	29 Amaziah, dies, age 53		²3223	780
171	1 Uzziah, 27 Jeroboam joint		3224	779
172	41 Jeroboam joint, dies		3238	765
173	Jotham born		¹3251	752
174	38 Azariah; 1 Zechariah, dies		²3261	742
175	39 Azariah, 1 Shallum, dies; Menahem Accession		²3262	741
176	Ahaz born, 10 Menahem, dies		²3272	731
177	50 Uzziah, 1 Pekahiah		3273	730
178	2 Pekahiah, dies		²3274	729
179	52 Azariah (Uzziah), dies, age 68; 1 Pekah		²3275	728
180	1 Jotham, 2 Pekah		3276	727
181	Hezekiah born		¹3283	720
182	16 Jotham, dies, age 40		²3291	712
183	1 Ahaz		3292	711
184	20 Pekah, dies [20 Jotham]		²3295	708
185	12 Ahaz, Hoshea Accession		3303	700
186	1 Hoshea		3305	698
187	16 Ahaz, dies, age 35; Hezekiah Accession, 3 Hoshea		²3307	697
188	1 Hezekiah		3308	695
189	4 Hezekiah, 7 Hoshea		3311	692
190	6 Hezekiah, 9 Hoshea		3313	690
191	14 Hezekiah		3321	682
192	Manasseh born		¹3325	678
193	29 Hezekiah, dies, age 53		²3336	667
194	1 Manasseh		3337	666
195	Amon born		3370	633
196	Josiah born		3386	617
197	55 Manasseh, dies, age 67		²3391	612
198	1 Amon		3392	611
199	2 Amon, dies, age 24		²3393	610
200	1 Josiah		3394	609
201	Jehoiakim born		3400	603
202	8 Josiah		3401	602
203	Jehoahaz born		¹3402	601

		A.M.	B.C.
204	12 Josiah	3405	598
205	13 Josiah	3406	597
206	18 Josiah	3411	592
207	Zedekiah born	¹3415	588
208	Jehoiachin born	¹3418	585
209	31 Josiah, dies, age 39	²3424	579
210	1 Jehoahaz, 1 Jehoiakim	3425	578
211	3 Jehoiakim	3427	576
212	4 Jehoiakim, 1 Nebuchadnezzar	3428	575
213	5 Jehoiakim, 2 Nebuchadnezzar	3429	574
214	6 Jehoiakim	3430	573
215	7 Nebuchadnezzar	3434	569
216	11 Jehoiakim, dies	²3435	568
217	1 Jehoiachin, 1 Zedekiah	3436	567
218	4 Zedekiah	3439	564
219	5 Zedekiah	3440	563
220	6 Zedekiah	3441	562
221	7 Zedekiah	3442	561
222	9 Zedekiah	3444	559
223	10 Zedekiah, 18 Nebuchadnezzar	3445	558
224	11 Zedekiah, sons die, 19 Nebuchadnezzar	²3446	557
		340,777	

Period 6. Captivity to Restoration,

		A.M.	B.C.
225	1 Captivity	3447	556
226	23 Nebuchadnezzar	3450	553
227	Darius born	¹3454	549
228	25 Captivity Jehoiachin	3460	443
229	27 Captivity Jehoiachin	3462	541
230	37 Captivity Jehoiachin, 1 Evil Merodach	3472	531
231	1 Darius	3515	488
232	2 Darius, Captivity ends	3516	487
	7 x 31 x 4 x 4 x 4 x 2	27,776	

Period 7. Restoration to the Christ.

			A.M.	B.C.
233	1	Cyrus, Seventy Weeks begin	3517	486
234	2	Cyrus	3518	485
235	3	Cyrus	3519	484
236		49 years of the 70 Weeks end	3565	438
237		Anna's husband dies	²3916	87
238		Annunciation by Gabriel	3998	5
239		The Lord born, 483 years end	¹3999	4
			26,032	

Period 8. Nativity to Pentecost.

		A.M.	B.C.
240	The Lord Jesus 12 Years old	4011	9
241	1 Tiberius	4015	13
242	15 Tiberius, the Lord Jesus 30, Year 1 of Ministry	4029	27
243	Year 2 of Ministry	4030	28
244	Year 3 of Ministry	4031	29
245	The Cross, Resurrection, and Ascension. Pentecost.	²4032	30
		24,148	
	(13 x 2 x 2 x 2 x 9 x 9 x 9 x 9) + 1	682,345	

Though the object of the Bible dates is clearly to enable the humble searcher to obtain a correct and consecutive Bible Chronology, the following is to be noted of Table I:

(1) It is indeed a complete register of all the events whose dates can be obtained from the Bible, but it does not give the dates of all the Bible events, it gives only a select List.

(2) The principle of selection is not the one usually looked for in such a Table. Thus in Periods I and II the purpose of a consecutive Chronology is accomplished by holding studiously only to the age of each father at the birth of only one son. Thus the age of Adam at the birth of Cain or Abel is withheld. But even this is not allowed to stand as a fixed rule. Noah's age is obtained at the birth two sons, likewise Abraham's. Of the sons of Jacob the choice of Joseph as the chronological link is indeed explicable both by his

character and as a type of the Blessed One. But the date of his death, which leads only to a chronological cul de sac was not required for **that** purpose. The Lord's life in the flesh having covered 33 years, or three **elevens**, it is conceivable that Joseph's death at 110, or 10 eleven's, is somehow connected with his typical character. This is strengthened by the death of Joshua, another type of the Lord, at the same age of 110. But unlike Joseph's, Joshua's birth year is not obtainable, while both the birth year and year 85 of Caleb, his fellow spy, are obtainable.

Nor does a reason readily appear for giving the age of Esau as 40 when marrying Judith, who as she is not mentioned before, neither is she mentioned thereafter. The dating of Ishmael's death at 137, of Levi and Amram at the same age, and of Kohath at 133, without enabling us to obtain the death years for these three, is not readily accounted for. Sarah's birth and death years are obtainable, but not those of Leah and Rachel. To this category belongs also Anna's husband, whose death is dated, though this event is one of only seven dated at all in a period of nearly 500 years. Anna's husband, like Esau's wife, as he is not heard before, neither is he heard of thereafter; this being in fact the case also with Anna herself.

And what to the mere wisdom of man must appear as the greatest anomaly of all is the fact that from the New Testament data not a single date can be obtained beyond the Ascension in 4032, though the whole history of the church of Christ is contained therein, from its Pentecostal rise in Acts to its dispensational end in Revelation, covering period of some 2,000 years, nearly half the time from Adam.

Of such seeming anomalies the reader will find not a few in Bible Chronology, which thus displays the same characteristics manifested in the Bible as a whole, God's one Spiritual Revelation, and in Creation, God's other, material, Revelation.

(3) A period of 2,520 years has now for decades been assumed by many writers as a chronological axiom for the Times of the Gentiles, with a whole apparatus of soli-lunar years, prophetic years of only 360 days each, with months of exactly 30 days, and more of the like. Now whatever truth there be in these notions,, they have either no support at all, or only the barest, in Scripture. The times of the Gentiles as a period are mentioned only once in Holy Writ, and without a glimmer of Chronology for it anywhere in the Book: the whole resting on the double meaning in **English only of** TIMES in the phrase, Seven times. The true rendering in Leviticus **sevenfold** pricks the

bubble of this being a prophecy of 360 sevens of years. As to soli-lunar years, which means sun-moon years, they are not found in the Bible, nor in every day speech. The sun measures years only, the moon measures months only, and a mixture of the two, like most mixtures, spoils both. For a year of 360 days the only warrant is the sole statement in the account of the Flood that 150 days made up five months. This, however, tells nothing about the other seven months, at the end of which the required five days may have been added to keep to the year of 365 days. Moreover, too little is known of the constitution of the ante-diluvian earth to make it safe to build aught more thereon than what is says: that certain specified five months that year covered 150 days. It may have been only every third, or every eighth, or even nineteenth year, of which this was true, there being no record of the then prevailing system of intercalation, if such was at all required. For if the present inclination of the axis of the earth of 23 degrees be the result of the cataclysm of the Flood year, a watery ring till then circling over the earth being let down thereon, the length of the year may have been affected thereby, so as to necessitate an intercalation needless hitherto.

(4) The Chronology of Table I is silent as to Daniel's seventieth week. It fixes the end of the 69 weeks at the birth of the Lord. The seventieth week, if already past now (in 1922) must have been fulfilled sometime between 4029, the beginning of the Ministry, and 4035, the end of that week of years. Not a single event, however, after the year of the Cross is dated (the writer had formed no opinion on the seventieth week as to whether it was past or future, when he began to set up this work). And no event which falls within those years, as recorded in the New Testament, has the remotest resemblance to the specifications laid down for the last of the 70 weeks. It **may** be in the past, but if so its determination becomes a matter of mere guesswork.

The Christian Era, with its A.D. notation, did not come into use till centuries after its beginning with the birth of the Lord, Dionysius the Little, the first to use it, began it with Year 754 of Rome in the belief that the Lord was born in that year. The Lord was born, however, before Herod's death. Now Josephus states that shortly before Herod's death not far from the Passover the moon was eclipsed in Judaea. This eclipse is astronomically fixed as in March of 4 B.C., or 750 Rome. The Christian Era was thus originally set four years too late, hence the anomaly of year 1 of the Christ having to be called year 4 before Christ.

Several dates of Scripture synchronize with dates in Profane history; thus:

4 Jehoiakim		3428	1 Nebuchadnezzar
10 Zedekiah		3445	18 Nebuchadnezzar
11 Zedekiah		3446	19 Nebuchadnezzar
37 Jehoiachin		3472	1 Evil Merodach
30 Lord		4029	15 Tiberius
9 x 9 x 2 x 11	17,820		54, or 9 x 2 x 3

As the Babylon dates are fixed by chronologers solely by these very synchronisms with the Bible, they are of no help for translating A.M. years into B.C. or A.D. years. The professed identification of certain years of antiquity by eclipses recorded by Ptolemy contains some logical fallacies which vitiate the results thus obtained.

The case is otherwise with the dates of Rome, synchronizing as they do with New Testament times. The years of Rome can be identified by eclipses beyond dispute. The battle of Actium is thus fixed at B.C. 31, and with it the reigns of Augustus. His death in A.D. 14 is likewise fixed by another eclipse, and with it the 5 years of the joint and sole reigns of Tiberius, his successor. It is thus that 15 Tiberius joint, or of Rome, is found to be 27 A.D. But Bible Chronology synchronizes 15 Tiberius with 4029. With this year thus identified as A.D. 27 every year from Adam is readily translated into A.D. and B.C. years.

TABLE II

In Table II are given the only 63 years out of the 245 in Table I which are regnal years of the kings of Judah and Israel. All these years are indeed common to both kingdoms, but not every year records necessarily events for both kingdoms. Thus 3056, or 3 Rehoboam, is also 3 Jeroboam; but 3 Rehoboam is specially mentioned in 2 Chronicles, while 3 Jeroboam is not mentioned either in Chronicles or Kings. Accordingly there is a blank in the Table for that year on the Israel side. Similarly, 3205, or 6 Omri, is also 32 Asa. But 6 Omri is named in Kings, while 32 Asa is named neither in Kings nor in Chronicles. Accordingly there is left a blank in the Table for that year on the Judah side; and so throughout. The reason for constructing this Table just thus appears in Part III.

In Part I, §§ 80—84, the manner of adjusting the dates for the two kingdoms has already in part been discussed. In this Table II every datum of

Kings and Chronicles for both kingdoms is harmonized: where there are apparent divergencies, they never extend for a whole year. And these divergencies (only three, in the case of three Israel kings of Jehoram, Menahem, and Pekah) are readily explained by the reigns of the kings of Israel not being uniformly reckoned as full or current, their data having been given for purposes other than a **consecutive** Chronology. See the years 3140, which one datum requires to be 4 Jehoram, and another 5; likewise Menahem's years 3263—3272, which give ten full years, but 11 current. The same is the case with Pekah's 20 years, which expire 3295, and yet his year 17 is 3291, instead of 3292. A difference in the beginning of the regnal year for Israel may also contribute to the divergence.

The case of Hoshea is apart by itself. Of the two beginnings of his reign one is clearly only his Accession, but according to the other data his first regnal year is not the next year, as in every other like case, but the year thereafter. Were more information vouchsafed here unto us about those turbulent times, the explanation would doubtless prove to be simple enough.

The only way, however, of thus harmonizing the two sets of data for Judah and Israel is by assuming some joint reigns, even in cases where the Book does not directly suggest it.. But as this expedient alone brings order here where all the others leave confusion, it is amply justified. By their fruits ye shall know them holds in literary criticism as well as in matters less pretentious, a fact too often forgotten by the theological professors of the day.

The numbers in Table II preceding its data are those of the places occupied by them in Table I. The superior figures preceding the numbers give their places in this Table.

KINGS OF ISRAEL AND JUDAH

		Judah		Israel
1	123	1 Rehoboam	3054	1 Jeroboam
2	124	3 Rehoboam	3056	
3	125	5 Rehoboam	3058	
4	126	17 Rehoboam	3070	
5	127	1 Abijam	3071	18 Jeroboam
6	128	3 Abijam, Asa Accession	3073	20 Jeroboam
7	129	1 Asa	3074	

8	130	2 Asa		3075	22 Jeroboam, 1 Nadab
9	131	3 Asa		3076	2 Nadab, 1 Baasha
10	133	10 Asa		3083	
11	134	15 Asa		3088	
12	135	26 Asa		3099	24 Baasha, 1 Elah
13	136	27 Asa		3100	2 Elah, 1 Omri
14	137	31 Asa		3104	5 Omri
15	138			3105	6 Omri
16	139	35 Asa		3108	
17	140	38 Asa		3111	Ahab's Accession, 12 Omri
18	141	39 Asa		3112	1 Ahab
19	142	41 Asa		3114	
20	143	1 Jehoshaphat		3115	4 Ahab
21	144	3 Jehoshaphat		3117	
22	146	17 Jehoshaphat		3131	20 Ahab, 1 Ahaziah, joint
23	147	18 Jehoshaphat		3132	1 Jehoram joint
24	148			3133	22 Ahab
25	149			3134	1 Ahaziah sole
26	150	1 Jehoram joint		3135	2 Ahaziah
27	151	2 Jehoram joint		3136	1 Jehoram sole
28	152	25 Jehoshaphat		3139	
29	153	1 Jehoram sole		3140	4—5 Jehoram
30	154	6 Jehoram		3145	
31	155	8 Jehoram Accession Ahaziah		3147	11—12 Jehoram
32	156	1 Ahaziah		3148	12 Jehoram
33	157	1 Attaliah		3149	1 Jehu
34	158	6 Attaliah		3154	
35	159	1 Joash		3155	7 Jehu
36	161			3176	28 Jehu
37	162	23 Joash		3177	1 Jehoahaz
38	163	37 Joash		3191	1 Joash joint
39	164			3193	17 Jehoahaz
40	165	40 Joash		3194	1 Joash sole

41	166	1 Amaziah	3195	2 Joash
42	167		3198	1 Jeroboam jt.
43	168	14 Amaziah	3208	
44	169	15 Amaziah	3209	16 Joash, 1 Jeroboam sole
45	170	29 Amaziah	3223	
46	171	1 Azariah	3224	27 Jeroboam jt.
47	172		3238	41 Jeroboam jt.
48	174	Azariah	3261	1 Zechariah
49	175	39 Azariah	3262	1 Shallum, 1 Menahem
50	176	Ahaz born	3272	10 Menahem
51	177	50 Azariah	3273	1 Pekahiah
52	178		3274	2 Pekahiah
53	179	52 Azariah	3275	1 Pekah
54	180	1 Jotham	3276	2 Pekah
55	182	16 Jotham	3291	16—17 Pekah
56	183	1 Ahaz	3292	
57	184	20 Jotham	3295	20 Pekah
58	185	12 Ahaz	3303	Hoshea Accession
59	186		3305	1 Hoshea
60	187	16 Ahaz, Hezekiah Accession	3307	3 Hoshea
61	188	1 Hezekiah	3308	
62	189	4 Hezekiah	3311	7 Hoshea
63	190	6 Hezekiah	3313	9 Hoshea

199,885, or 7 x 5 x 5711

PART III

PART III

The Numeric Phenomena

1. In Parts I and II the data for Bible Chronology are dealt with on their own merits. If correctly given, and rightly interpreted, they stand; if incorrectly given, or misinterpreted, they fall. The facts and their interpretation as given there accordingly speak for themselves. Parts I and II are thus complete in themselves, independent of the question whether the Bible is verbally inspired or not.

2. But for those to whom the Bible has already accredited itself as the Book from God, or to those even who are still willing to listen to the evidence for its inspiration, Part III furnishes the evidence that here at last is the true Chronology not only of the Bible, but of all history, of the human race, and the earth it dwells in. That for which the much abused word Science is meant to stand is good, and Archeology is good, and Assyriology, and Egyptology; and the Ptolemy Canon is good, and the eclipses recorded therein and elsewhere. And so are the monuments, inscriptions, and coins. And Herodotus is good, and Ctesias and Xenophon, as are also Sanchoniathon and Berosus and Manetho and Firdusi and the Sedar Olam. To the extent that they agree with the Bible they are indeed invaluable. But to the extent that they disagree, and irreconcilably so, they are doomed. For in these there is always the element of error in observation or report, or transmission of the data, or even in the data themselves. And this holds also of the one evidence that has hitherto been deemed unimpeachable—even of eclipses.

3. Even of Eclipses. Once indeed established, the testimony of an eclipse as to a date is final: since the very heavens would have to be rent asunder ere an eclipse properly observed and reported can be belied. Such an eclipse, however, it is certain, will never conflict with true Bible Chronology. But the

true adjustment of eclipses to the events they are supposed to attest by folk living long after their occurrence, is a wholly different matter.

4. Thus Herodotus states that in the midst of a battle between Lydians and Medes an eclipse of the sun took place, which caused the frightened combatants to make peace at once. The eclipse is said to have been foretold by Thales, the first in history to predict such an event, unless a certain Chinese tradition be authentic. Herodotus, not a contemporary, reports this eclipse at second, if not third, or even tenth hand. As the battle was at the Halys, astronomers set out to identify it: a total eclipse of the sun at a specified place, and limited only to certain hours of the day—apparently a simple task for giant scientists. After much wavering between, say, 580 and 615 B.C., it was at last allowed to settle down as an astronomic fixity for 595. On this as a basis elaborate systems of chronology and history were forthwith built with Gibraltaresque solidity, and a confidence duly befitting such solid foundation. And this assured result of the most infallible of sciences thus stood indeed for a goodly century and a half, until the justly authoritative Ideler gave it short shrift indeed in one lone still shorter paragraph; and forthwith history and chronology based thereon made a rather inglorious exit.

Ideler, of course, may be right; and the writer is ready enough to follow him here—provisionally. But it **may be** not yet an assured result of Science; it is not even science. It is at most a very probable supposition, but even a probable supposition still remains mere supposition.

5. This caution in the presence of even an Ideler is all the more needful, because it was he who with the support of the great Kepler set the birth of the Lord several years before 4 B.C. In the year of their choice remarkable conjunctions of three planets took place. This, say Kepler and Ideler, is what guided the Magi to the Bethlehem babe. Matthew says a star. Kepler was not halted by this and the great Ideler satisfied himself that to a person with weak eyes the several planets would probably appear as one star, though at no time were the planets nearer to each other than the moon's diameter. But Patchard, who unlike the writer, could go over the elaborate calculations of Kepler and Ideler, found that the path of those conjunction planets was such that much of the time they could not be seen at all on the road to Bethlehem. And thus exit this time most ingloriously a scientific verity established indubitably with the whole astronomic apparatus of a Kepler and an Ideler.

And if this is true of two such modern giants, how much greater the need of caution in the case of Ptolemy, with his distance of centuries from those whose labours he largely only transcribes.

6. Thus it comes to pass that even eclipses, especially the ancient Ptolemy eclipses, are for the present out of court before Bible Chronology as established by Numerics, however useful they be as a basis for discussion.

For the evidence furnished by Bible Numerics is such that even the disruption of the heavens need not disturb it. When Emerson was told by a Millerite of his day that the world was coming to an end, he answered that this did not concern him, since he could get on without it. And Emerson was only a Pagan. Christian, however, looks not only without dismay at the day when the heavens being on fire shall be dissolved, and the elements shall melt with fervent heat, he actually looks for it with hope. But the nature of Bible Numerics is such that a rational man would have to be rent asunder himself ere he could deny the force of their demonstration. The human mind is so constructed that when brought face to face with the fact however unwelcome that A equals B, and B equals C, he **must** draw the conclusion that A equals C. Now all Bible Numerics, in its vast variety of the phenomena, demonstrations, and methods, is only a symphonic variation of the fundamental theme that if A equals B, and B equals C, A also equals C.

Anti-Christian Scholarship ignores Numerics because it does not wish them to be true. It hates the Bible here too much. Christians ignore Numerics because they do not love the Bible enough.

7. If the reader will now turn to Table 1, pages 155—164, he will see that the 245 dates therein alone obtainable from the Bible naturally fall into the following periods made by the Bible itself:

TABLE III

1	Adam to Flood	1656	0—1656
2	Flood to Covenant	451	1657—2107
3	Covenant to Exodus	430	2108—2537
4	Exodus to Temple	480	2538—3017
5	Temple to Captivity	429	3018—3446
6	Captivity to Restoration	70	3447—3516
7	Restoration to Advent	483	3517—3999
8	Advent to Ascension	33	4000—4032
		4032	20285 24310

	4,032 is 7 x 24 x 24, or 7 x 9 x 8 x 8.		
	20,285 is (7 x 7 x 9 x 2 x 23) - 1		
	24,310 is 11 x 13 x 17 x 2 x 5		

Period 1 is determined by the data in Genesis 5, and Noah's age at the Flood. Period 2 is. determined by those Genesis 11, and the age of Abraham at the Covenant, fixed with the aid of Stephen's address in Acts 7. Period 3 is determined by Paul in Gal. 3: 17, and Ex. 12: 41. Period 4 is determined by 1 Kings 6: 1. Period 5, by the various data in 1 and 2 Kings, and 1 and 2 Chron. Period 6, by Jer. 25: 11—12, Zech. 1: 12; 2 Chron. 36: 21. Period 7, by Dan. 9, 2 Chron. 36: 22, and Ezra 1: 1. Period 8, by Luke 3: 23, and the passovers in John.

Of these 8 periods 7 are covered by the Old Testament, the Scriptural number for Completeness of one series, the Old; the eighth is covered by the New, 8 being the number for a new order, the octave, beginning of another series, a new creation.

8. The only Bible books from which the data for a Bible Chronology are obtainable are: Genesis, Exodus, Numbers, Deuteronomy, Joshua, Judges, and 2 Samuel, 1 and 2 Kings, Jeremiah, Ezekiel, Zechariah, Daniel, Ezra, 1 and 2 Chronicles, Luke, John, Acts and Galatians. In other books there are indeed also dated events, but not dated so as to enable us to place them safely in the list of Bible dates. Thus Haggai names 2 Darius Hystaspes, and Nehemiah gives 20 Artaxerxes; but from the Bible we cannot say in what year from Adam either Darius or Artaxerxcs began to reign. For a Bible Chronology these dates are thus of no help. Now the number of the Bible books thus alone available is 21, or 3 sevens (Feature 1); of which those used for the eight periods (as enumerated in § 7) are 14 in number, or 2 sevens; leaving seven for those not so used (Feature 2).

9. The 8 periods cover 4,032 years, or 576 sevens (Feature 3). These 8 periods are divided into two unequal halves thus: 3 are numbers with zeros: 430, 480, 70; the other five are without zeros. With reference to this fact the sum of the years covered by these 8 periods, 4032, or 576 sevens, is divided thus: the 3 zero numbers have 980, or 7 x 7 x 4 x 5, a multiple of seven sevens (Feature 4); and the no-zero numbers have 3052, or 7 x 4 x 109, or 436 sevens (Feature 5). And this division, moreover, is not only by sevens, but by 4 sevens.

10. Among the periods the 4032 years are distributed thus: Periods 1–2

cover 2107 years, or 7 x 7 x 43. This number has this peculiarity: It is itself a multiple of seven sevens (Feature 6); and the sum of the figures of its factors is 21, or 3 sevens (Feature 7). Periods 3—4 cover 910 years, or 130 sevens (Feature 8); Period 6 covers 70 years, or 7 x 2 x, 5, a number which like 2107 (see Feature 6 and 7) has also this distinction: It is itself 10 sevens (Feature 9), with the sum of its factors 14, or 2 sevens (Feature 10), and the sum of its figures seven (Feature 11). Period 7 covers 483 years, or 69 sevens (Feature. 12); leaving for the other two periods 462 years, or 66 sevens (Feature 13).

11. The number of dates in these 8 periods is 245, or 7 x 7 x 5, a multiple of seven (Feature 14) sevens (Feature 15): of which Periods 1—2 have each 21, or 3 sevens (Feature 16); Period 3 has 28, or 4 sevens (Feature 17); Period 4 has 49, or seven (Feature 183 sevens (Feature 19); and Period 7 has 7 (Feature 20); leaving for the remaining periods 119, or 17 sevens (Feature 21).

This distribution into sevens by periods has this further peculiarity: Of the 8 periods each of the first four has for the number of its years a multiple of seven. Then there is a break in this regularity, and only one of the other four periods has for its number of years a multiple of seven. Now the first four periods, each of which is a multiple of seven, have together 119 years, or 17 sevens. Accordingly, the three periods that are not multiples of seven have also between them 119 years, or 17 sevens.

There is thus still a definite regularity in the very midst of apparent regularity. The number of years, 245, or 35 sevens, is an **uneven** number of sevens, and cannot therefore be divided into two equal halves. But the symmetry is nevertheless kept, thus:

Periods with sevens	119, or 7 x 17
Periods without sevens	119, or 7 x 17
Period by itself	7, or 7 x 1

12. The same method of dividing into halves as nearly as the **odd** number 245 allows it (see § 9) is followed also with regard to the distinction kept up between the birth and death years on the one hand and the other years on the other. In Table I the birth and death years are specially distinguished by (^{1}) and (^{2}) respectively; and in Enoch's case by (*). Now with respect to this the 245 years in Table I are divided thus: The births and deaths (the Translation of Enoch included, it being a departure from this life), are 126, or 18 sevens; leaving for the other years 119, or 17 sevens (Feature 22), the 35 sevens of

245 being divided into 17 and 18, the two nearest halves.

The 126 years of births, deaths and Translation are in their turn divided thus: the deaths alone (with Enoch's year) have 77, or 11 sevens; the births and the births and deaths in the same year have 49. or seven (Feature 23) sevens (Feature 24).

13. In Table II, page 170, are given the years from the beginning of the kingdom of Israel under Jeroboam to its end under Hoshea. With respect to this the 245 Bible years are divided thus: the kingdom of Israel spans over 63 dates, or 9 sevens; leaving for the others 182, or 26 sevens (feature 25).

14. The years with which these 8 periods begin (Table 3) have for the sum of their figures 98, or 2 sevens (Feature 26) of sevens (Feature 27). The sum of these years themselves, 20,285, is itself not a multiple of seven, but it is neighhour to 20,286, or 7 x 7 x 9 x 2 x 23, a multiple not only of seven, but of seven sevens, combined moreover with 2 nine and 23, for which numbers see below. The bearing of **neighbour-hood** here will be explained below: meanwhile, though not reckoned as additional numeric features, the reader may bear them in mind for future reference.

15. Of the great landmarks of Bible history the Covenant, the Temple, and the Cross have for their years each a multiple seven: 2107, 3017, and 4032, each of these years ending a period. With the other dates that are equally landmarks, though not found at the end of a period. we have:

TABLE IV

1	Translation of Enoch	987, or 7 x 141
2	Birth of Peleg	1757, or 7 x 251
3	The Covenant	2107, or 7 x 301
4	Joseph Egypt's ruler	2289, or 7 x 327
5	Years of Plenty end	2296, or 7 x 328
6	Moses born	2457, or 7 x 351
7	Moses and Aaron die	2576, or 7 x 368
8	Division of Land	2583, or 7 x 369
9	Oppressions begin	2611, or 7 x 373
10	Deliverance by Ehud	2730, or 7 x 390
11	Jephthah judge	2877, or 7 x 411

12	Deliverance of Mizpeh	2947, or 7 x 421
13	David sole king	2975, or 7 x 425
14	Temple begun	3017, or 7 x 431
15	Temple finished	3024, or 7 x 432
16	Samaria besieged	3311, or 7 x 473
17	Nebuchadnezzar's dream	3430, or 7 x 490
18	Jerusalem besieged	3444, or 7 x 492
19	Jehoiachin Captivity ends	3472, or 7 x 496
20	The Lord 12	4011, or 7 x 573
21	The Cross	4032, or 7 x 576

16. What is noticeable about this Table is this: In 245 numbers, or 35 sevens, 35 may be expected to be multiples of seven, since one number in seven has a chance of being a multiple of seven. Accordingly, among the 245 numbers of Table I there are 33 multiples of seven. And so far all is normal. But just 21 of these, or 3 sevens (Feature 28), are marked events, as a glance at Table IV shows. Some, like the birth and death of Moses, are events seen at once as marked, others appear so only on reflection, but marked events they all are. Thus at Peleg's birth it is noted that in his days the earth was divided. Whatever the event, whether a catastrophe or not, the Spirit thus singled it out from other births. Ehud's deliverance is thus likewise made noticeable by being connected with a rest of 80 years, where the others are only 40. The sieges of Samaria and Jerusalem are the marked years rather than their captures, because once surrounded their doom was sealed. And so with the other numbers.

§ 17. One of these 21 numbers stands out specially. At the interpretation of his dream Nebuchadnezzar was told by Daniel, Thou art the head of gold. With him then as head of the Image the Times of the Gentiles were thus divinely appointed to begin. This was in 3430. But this is 7 x 7 x 7 x 2 x 5, itself seven (Feature 29) sevens (Feature 30) of seven (Feature 31), with the sum of its factors 28, or 4 sevens (Feature 32). Below it will be seen that some of these other years have also striking features of their own. For the present only one need be pointed out: The siege of Samaria, being the final abandoning of the kingdom of Israel by Jehovah, is in 3311, or 7 x 43 x 11, the 7 x 43 being the very combination already found in the year of the Covenant, 2107, or 7 x 7 x 42. The 43, moreover, will be seen below to have a special place in Chronology.

18. Hitherto Table I with its 245 numbers has been examined as a whole. Of its 8 periods only one is covered by the New Testament, the rest are covered by the Old. Let us examine the years from the first Adam to the second Adam, the Old Testament periods by themselves.

The number of these periods is seven (Feature 33). The seven Period totals (see at end of each Period in Table 1), which are: 20,787, 40,248, 63,840, 138,737, 340,777, 27,776, and 26,032.

19. This enumeration of the features of seven in the 245 years of Table I is not exhaustive, it is only scratching the surface: they are not the most striking that could be presented. They are given here because they best serve the writer's immediate purpose toward the reader. Thus the 12 Sabbatic years of Table I, not given in Table IV, are:

2618	3080	3136	3283
2814	3108	3262	3325
3073	3115	3276	3402

The sum of the 21 Sabbatic years in Table IV is 58,933, a multiple of seven; but the sum of its figures is 28, or 4 sevens (Feature 34). Compare Features 7, 11, 26, 27 and 32. Of the 245 years in Table I, or 35 sevens, 77, or 11 sevens, are with zeros (Feature 35). Of these 77 zero years 11, or one seventh, are sabbatic, namely: 2107, 2730. 3017, 3024, 3073, 3080, 3108, 3402, 3430, 4011, 4032. Their sum is a multiple of seven, and the sum of their figures is 112, or 16 sevens (Feature 36).

20. These 36 sevens are in Table I either undesigned, mere coincidence, just by chance, or they are put there by some intelligence, are designed. If not designed, it is chance, if not chance it is designed. This is positively the first FACT which the reader **must** accept.

Now the chance for anything merely happening, being undersigned, accidental, is readily calculated. Thus, What is the chance for the above 36 features of sevens being undesigned, a mere coincidence, is the same as asking, What is the chance for any 36 numbers being multiples of seven? Now the chance for any number being a multiple of 7 is for:

1	1 in	7
2	1 in	49
3	1 in	343
4	1 in	2401
5	1 in	16,807
6	1 in	117,649
7	1 in	823,543
8	1 in	5,764,801
9	1 in	40,353,607
10	1 in	282,475,249
11	1 in	1,977,326,743
12	1 in	13,841,287,201
13	1 in	96,889,010,407
14	1 in	678,223,072,849
15	1 in	4,747,561,509,943
16	1 in	33,232.930,569,601
17	1 in	232,630,513,987,207
18	1 in	1,628,413,597,910,449
19	1 in	11,398,895,185,373,143
20	1 in	79,792,266,297,612,001
21	1 in	558,545,864,023,284,007
22	1 in	3,909,821,048,582,988,049
23	1 in	27,368,747,340,080,916,343

21. This calculation extending only to two thirds of the 36 under discussion reaches already a number of **twenty figures**. So that the chance for any 23 features of sevens just happening together is only one in some 27 **millions of a million millions**. The chance for 36 features of sevens thus to happen together is only one in a number of **thirty-one figures**.

In the above calculation the largest number possible is allowed for the chance of these 36 sevens being here undesigned, accidental. Their actual chance here is much smaller. This the chance for any multiple of seven, say 98, being divided into two multiples of seven is not one in 14, even though 98 is 14 sevens. For it can be divided only into these sets: 7 and 91: 14 and 84; 21 and 77; 28 and 70; 35 and 63; 42 and 56; 49 and 49. As these sets are only seven, the chance for such a division is not one in 14, but only one in 49. As there are several such features among the 36 enumerated, the chance for their being undesigned is to that extent much lessened. The same is true of the several numbers that are multiples not only of seven, but of 4 sevens. The chance for any two numbers being multiples of 4 sevens, or 28, is not merely one in 49 (as it has been uniformly reckoned in the above calculation), but only one or 28 x 28, or 784. And the same is true of other features.

The question may be put in another form thus. A bag containing 42 apples drops off a moving cart, and all the 42 apples roll out into the street. What is the chance for the likelihood of the 47 apples rolling out so as to form themselves into six rows of seven each, or of seven rows of six each? The natural answer is, They have no chance at all for such self-arrangement, it is impossible. Should, therefore, the apples be found thus arranged, there can be only one verdict thereover: Some one thus designedly arranged them. Likewise, the 36 features of sevens enumerated above are not in Table I by chance: some one designedly put them there. **An elaborate design of sevens thus runs through the 245 years alone deducible from the Bible.**

22. If the reader will now turn to the end of Period 8 in Part II, he will see that the sum of 245 years is 682,345, neighhour of 682,344 or 13 x 2 x 2 x 2 x 9 x 9 x 9 x 9, a multiple of thirteen (Feature 1), divided thus: Period I has 20,787, or 13 x 13 x 41 x 3, a multiple of thirteen thirteens (Feature 2); Period II has 40,248, or 13 x 43 x 2 x 2 x 2 x 3 x 3 or 3,096 thirteens (Feature 3). The number of years in period V, 27,776, or 7 x 31 x 4 x 4 x 4 x 2, is a multiple of seven only. But while itself not a multiple of thirteen, the sum of its factors is 52, or 4 thirteens (Feature 4). And the same is the case with Period VII: the sum of its years, 26,032. while itself not a multiple of thirteen, has for the sum of its figures thirteen (Feature 5).

23. The first dated year in the Bible is 130, or 10 thirteens (Feature 6). The sum of the 8 years with which the 8 periods end (Table 3, page 162) is 24,310, or 1870 thirteens (Feature 7).

The years obtained from Genesis are in their turn divided thus: To the Flood, 20,787, or 13 x 13 x 3 x 41, itself a multiple of 13 x 13, with 70 for the sum of its factors, or 10 sevens. The years beyond the Flood have 38,493, or 13 x 3 x 3 x 7 x 47, a multiple of thirteen (Feature 8) as well as of seven. The division here is moreover not only by thirteens, but by 13 x 3, and with this distinction: In the first number the 13 is doubled as a factor, in the second it is the 3 that is doubled.

24. The chance for any number being a multiple of thirteen is given on the next page. For these 8 features of thirteens to be accidental, undesigned, the chance is only one in over 815 millions.

And this enumeration of thirteens is also, as in the case of the sevens, not exhaustive, it is only scratching the surface.

An elaborate design of thirteens as well as of sevens thus runs through the 245 years of Table I.

25. The sum of the 245 Bible years, 682,345, neighbor of 682,344 or 13 x 8 x 9 x 9 x 9 x 9, is a multiple of 8 x 9 or 72 (Feature 1) as well as of 13. Accordingly it is divided thus: Period 2 has 40248, or 13 x 72 x 43, and the other periods have 642,097, neighbour of 642,096 or 72 x 13 x 7 x 7 x 7 x 2, the division being here by 13 seventy-twos (Feature 2), combined in the second number, moreover, with seven sevens of sevens. The time covered by Bible Chronology, 4032 years, is 7 x 72 x 8, a multiple of seventy-two (Feature 3) as well as of seven. And this is divided thus: Period 1 has 1656 years, or 23 seventy-twos; and the other 7 periods have 2376, or 33 seventy-twos (Feature 4).

The Chance for any number being a multiple of thirteen is for

1	1 in	13
2	1 in	169
3	1 in	2,197
4	1 in	28,561
5	1 in	371,293
6	1 in	4,826,809
7	1 in	62,748,517
8	1 in	815,730,721
9	1 in	10,604,499,373
10	1 in	137,858,491,849
11	1 in	1,792,160,394,037
12	1 in	23,298,085,122,481
13	1 in	302,875,106,592,253

| 14 | 1 in | 3,937,376,385,699,289 |
| 15 | 1 in | 51,185,893,014,090,757 |

Again: The Temple was finished in the year 3024, or 72 x 7 x 6; thence to the Cross, when its veil was rent as a token of being disowned henceforth of God, is 1008 years, or 7 x 72 x 2, the division being by 2 sevens of seventy-two (Feature 5).

As the chance for these 5 Features of seventy-twos being undesigned is only one in 1,934,917,632, one in nearly two thousand millions, design of 8 x 9, or 72, thus also runs through the 245 Bible years as well as a design of seven and of thirteen. And neither is this enumeration exhaustive.

26. Looking once more to the 7 periods from Adam to the Christ by themselves, covering as they do the whole Bible Chronology lacking only 33 years, we find that they cover 3999 years, a number unexpected: since man would have made it an even 4,000. But 3999 is 3 x 31 x 43. The sum of its factors is 77, itself 11 sevens, with 14, or 2 sevens as the sum of its own figures, 7, 7. The sum of the figures be factors 3, 31, 43, is also 14, or 2 sevens: of which the first two have 7, and the third has 7. This number 3999, though itself not a multiple of seven, is nevertheless found to be marked with 4 features of sevens, one for every one of its four figures. This, however, is not the primary distinction of this number. It is 93 forty-threes (Feature 1), divided thus: To the Covenant, 2107, 43 x 7 x 7, or a multiple of 43 and seven sevens; Covenant to the Exodus, 430, or 43 x 2 x 5, itself 10 forty-threes (Feature 2), and the sum of its own figures is 7, and that of its factors 14, or 2 sevens. From the Exodus to the Christ 1462, or 34 forty-threes (Feature 3). From the Temple to the Captivity the number of years is 429, itself 33 thirteens, but neighhour of 430, or 10 forty-threes. Period II, which ends with Year 2107, or 43 x 7 x 7, has for the sum of its years 40,248, or 43 x 13 x 9 x 8 a multiple of 43 (Feature 4), as well as of 13 and 72, or 8 x 9.

27. It has just been noted that the 429 years of Period 5 is itself a multiple of thirteen, but is neighbour of 430, or 10 forty-threes. The same is the case with the first year of Bible Chronology, 130. It is itself 10 thirteens, but is also, neighbour to 129, or 3 forty-threes.

A scheme of forty-threes, as well as of 7, 13, and 72, thus runs through the 245 Bible years.

§ 28. The writer is concerned at present only with the demonstration that several most elaborately varied numeric designs are present in the 245 Bible years. Seven is a number which is stamped on the whole Bible visible even to the weakest eye. But the other numbers are also frequent therein, though not so visibly. Thus the three monarchs of Babylon, Media, and Persia, who had specially to do with the Captivity and the Restoration, are Nebuchadnezzar, Darius, and Cyrus (without the **Vav**). Their Value in the Hebrew is 1652, itself a multiple of seven, it being 7 x 4 x 59, with the sum of its figures 14, or 2 sevens; and the sum of its factors 70, or 7 x 2 x 5, again 10 sevens, with 14, or 2 sevens, as the sum of its factors; this Value 1652, or 236 sevens, is divided thus: the Place value has 196, or 4 sevens of sevens, and the numeric value is 1456, or 7 x 13 x 4 x 4, itself 208 sevens, with the sum of its factors 28, or 4 sevens.

29. This design of sevens thus seen to run through these three names which form a class by themselves, is indeed to be expected in view of the whole structure of the Bible being permeated with sevens. But what is noticeable here is that the Numeric value 1456 is a multiple of 13 as well as of 7. And its 13 x 7 x 4 x 4 are divided thus: Nebuchadnezzar has 416, or 13 x 4 x 4 x 2. Darius and Cyrus have 1040, or 13 x 4 x 4 x 5, the divisions being not only by thirteens, but by 16 thirteens. Moreover, the numeric value of Darius is 520, or 40 thirteens, and that of Cyrus is also 520. The Place Value of Cyrus is moreover 52, or 4 thirteens.

30. The same phenomenon is duplicated in the case of Jacob, and his father Isaac on the one hand, and his beloved son Joseph on the other. The three patriarchs have together a numeric value of 546, or 7 x 13 x 6, again the combination of both seven and thirteen. And this numeric value 546 or 7 x 13 x 6 (the same also is the number of words in the Vocabulary of the Epistle of James, with an elaborate scheme of sevens and thirteens forming its warp and woof) is divided thus: Jacob himself has 182, or twice 7 x 13; and his father and son have 364, or 4 times seven thirteens. And of this number Isaac has 208, or 13 x 4 x 4, itself 16 thirteens, with the sum of its factors 21, or 3 sevens; Joseph has 156, or thrice 4 thirteens, the division being not only by thirteens, but by 4 thirteens.

31. It was just noted parenthetically that the Epistle of James has an elaborate design of thirteens running through it. This is an in nowise isolated phenomenon in the New Testament, is quite frequent in fact in the whole Bible, only it is not so readily perceived as the seven. Thus the vocabulary to the first chapter of Matthew has 130 words, or 10 thirteens (Compare the 130 of the first Bible date); the first two chapters of Matthew have 897 words, or

13 x 23 x 3, itself 69 thirteens, with the sum of its factors 39, or 3 thirteens with schemes of thirteens and twenty-threes running, through them.

A reason thus appears for the frequency of the sevens and the thirteens in Bible Chronology: they are only the duplication of the phenomena usual throughout the Bible as a whole.

32. Before leaving the thirteens, however, the following fact is to be noted. The **scientific** Vocabulary of the New Testament[1] has 5304 words, or 13 x 17 x 2 x 2 x 2 x 3, itself a multiple of thirteen, with the sum of its factors 39, or 3 thirteens. In view of what has just been said this is indeed to be expected. But the thirteen is here combined **seventeen**, as is also the case with the sum of the years with which the eight periods end (Table 3), 24,310 being a multiple of 13 x 17. Now 17 is indeed often found to be the basis of numeric design in Scripture similar to 7 and 13. At present, however, is merely to be noted the peculiar relation which it holds to thirteen, its immediate predecessor among prime numbers. Accordingly seventeen itself wilt oft be found in the **neighbourhood** of thirteen, when not actually combined with it. This is the case for example with Jacob and his beloved Joseph. He lives 147 years, or 3 sevens of sevens, is 91 at Joseph's birth, or 7 x 13. He is 130, or 10 thirteens when re-united with his beloved son. And he lives thereafter with Joseph just 17 years. The numeric value of **Iakob** in the New Testament, in the Greek, is 833, or 7 x 7 x 17: already remarkable enough; but it is neighbour of 832 or 13 x 8 x 8. In like manner Joseph is sold into Egypt at 17; 13 years thereafter, at 30 he is Egypt's ruler, and is re-united with his father at 39, or 3 thirteens. Accordingly, the same phenomena appear

---

[1] There is at present no such scientific Vocabulary. The writer had to make one for his own use. The numeric phenomena of the Bible vocabularies come into view only when they are constructed on principles hitherto ignored by grammarians and lexicographers. Thus the verb **go** has no past tense of its own, and **went** supplies it. But it is not a true account of the matter to say that went is the past of **go**. It is only used as such. The true account of the matter is that **go** is a defective verb, and its missing forms are taken from another word. In a scientific vocabulary **go** and **went** would be reckoned not as one word, but as two, defective, verbs.

Now in the Greek such cases are quite numerous: **eltho** and **erchomai** for GO; **fero** and **enenko** for BRING. Again: wise, wisely are treated as two vocabulary words now by men, but not by God in His Book. **Sofos** and **sofohs** are in the New Testament not two different words, but two forms of the same vocabulary word. And the same is true of the Hebrew in certain parallel cases of verbs and their verbal nouns. With this correction of the modern methods of Bible Vocabularies present remarkable Numerics. Without it, confusion.

Thus it comes to pass that the writer had to construct his own Concordance and Vocabularies for his work, which requires the utmost accuracy to the slightest detail.

also in Chronology. The most notable event in Period I is Enoch's Translation in 987. This, as is to be expected, is 141 sevens; but it is neighhour not only of 988, or 13 x 19 x 4, or 76 thirteens (this too is to be expected after what has been expounded above), but also of 986, or 58 seventeens. In other words, the date of the first of the only two Translations in the Bible is stamped not only with seven, but by means of neighbourhood also with 13 and 17 (and incidentally also with the very next prime number, 19): 7, 13, 17, 19.

33. The same phenomenon is duplicated in the prime event of Period 2, the Covenant, in 2107. This is itself, as was to be expected here, a multiple of seven, and even of seven sevens, it being 7 x 7 x 43. But it is neighbour of 2106 on the one side, or 13 x 9 x 9 x .2, a multiple not only of 13, but combined with nine nines (compare the sum of the 245 Bible years). The other neighbour, 2108, is 124 seventeens.

Similarly, the Law was given in 2537. It was fulfilled on the Cross, and the shadow then became Gospel light, in 4032. The Law thus lasted 1495 years (the same as the numeric value of the Hebrew alphabet, the language of the Old Covenant), or 115 thirteens, this too, as is to be expected. But it is neighbour of 1496, or 17 x 11 x 2 x 2 x 2, itself 88 seventeens, with the sum of its factors 34, or 2 seventeens. See also § § 42, 45, 48.

§ 34. At the bottom of page 160 it is seen that the sum of the years in Period 4 is 138,737, or 8,161 seventeens, but neighbour of 138,736, a multiple of thirteen. The last date of Genesis is 2369, the death of Joseph. The last date of Exodus is 2538, year 2 from the Exodus. Their sum is 4907, or 701 sevens, as might be expected. But their difference is 169, itself 13 x 13; but neighbour of 170, or 10 seventeens; and of 168, or 24 sevens: 7, 13, 17, 24, the last three being the very factors of 5304, the number of words in the Vocabulary of the New Testament.

Again: If the number of years in each of the seven periods to the Incarnation be multiplied by its order number, we have:

```
1656 x 1 is 1656
 451 x 2 is  902
 430 x 3 is 1290
 480 x 4 is 1920
 429 x 5 is 2145
  70 x 6 is  420
 483 x 7 is 3381
```

The sum thus obtained is 11,714, neighbour of 11,713, or 13 x 17 x 53; divided thus: the even numbers have 6188, or 7 x 13 x 17 x 4; the odd numbers have 5526, neighbour of 5525, or 13 x 17 x 25, the division being by 13 seventeen combined in one case moreover with seven. And thus the writer might go on for pages.

35. In §26 it was noted that a scheme of 72 also runs through the 682,345 years of Bible Chronology. The first New Testament section, Matt. 1:1-17, the genealogy of the Lord Jesus, has a vocabulary of 72 words, thus corresponding perhaps to the years in Period I, 1656, which is 72 x 23.

Seventy-two is however 3 twenty-fours, and the 4032 years which cover Bible Chronology are accordingly 7 x 24 x 24. Now the number of words in the New Testament Vocabulary is 5304, a multiple off 13, 17, 24. The 24 courses in the Temple worship, the 24 Elders in Revelation, and others that could be named, show thus a reason for the seventy-twos and twenty-fours, not uncommon elsewhere in the Scriptures, also appearing in Bible Chronology.

36. And the same is true of the scheme of 43 found to be running through Bible Chronology (§ § 27—28). The very first word in the Bible B'RAYSHITH, **In Beginning**, has its value 989 or 23 forty-threes. Of the seven words of the first verse of the Bible one only, the untranslatable ETH, is used twice. Its two occurrences have a value of 860 or 20 forth-threes. **Elohim**, God, has a numeric value of 86, or 2 forty-threes. This one verse of only seven words thus displays three features of forty-threes. In the next verse **Tohu Vabohu**, Waste and Void, found only twice elsewhere in the Bible, has a numeric value of 430, or 10 forty-threes. In Dan. 12: 11 the number of days is 1290, or 30 forty-threes. Abraham is 86, or 43 x 2 at the birth of Ishmael, his first son. And more of the like.

A reason thus appears for every one of the four numeric schemes permeating the 245 Bible years, these being merely the same phenomena found elsewhere in the Bible.

37. The only years deducible from the Bible, 245 in number are thus **demonstrated** to have most elaborate numeric designs running through them put there clearly by an—Intelligence.

The writer is almost ashamed to have to emphasise the word

DEMONSTRATE. But there are even well-meaning Christian folk, who flatter themselves with the notion that because the matter is not demonstrated to **them**, they are free to adjudge it as not demonstrated at all.

38. No single mortal could have successfully carried through this design in even one book during a life-time of say a hundred years, with all these 100 years given solely thereto.

39. Now that these Numerics were put here by a super-human intelligence is clear from the simple consideration that they extend over 66 hooks written by 33 folk, with some 1600 years between the first and last writers. What has thus elsewhere been demonstrated concerning the Bible as a whole and its every part is now found to be true also of its Chronology as a whole. It now remains to be shown that this is equally true of its parts.

Of the 8 separate Periods some have Numerics on the very surface, to be seen almost on inspection. Thus Period I has these Numerics of its own: Its 21 years, or 3 sevens, have for their sum 20787, multiple of thirteen thirteens, being 13 x 13 x 3 x 41. The sum of these factors is 70, or 10 sevens. The sum 20787 itself is divided thus: the birth years marked (1) have 4784, or 368 thirteens; leaving for the other years 16003, or 1231 thirteens. The first patriarch to live in this Period is Adam; the last to die is Methuselah; the only one who survives the Flood is Noah. Their dates are 130, 687, 930, 1056, 1656. Their sum is 4459, 7 x 7 x 7 x 13. The same sevens and thirteens already met so abundantly before. And very much more of the like.

40. The sum of the years of Period I has just been seen to be a multiple of 41 as well as of 13. Now though Genesis closes with the year 2369, the death of Joseph, which is date Number 65, or 5 thirteens, in Table I, not all these dates are obtainable from Genesis. The date of Abraham's birth is learned only from the remark of Stephen in Acts 7 that Abram was 75 after his father's death. Every date therefore affected by the age of Abraham is obtained outside of Genesis. There are 24 such dates: leaving just 41 for the number of dates obtainable from Genesis alone.

These dates derived from Genesis alone (Table V below) have elaborate numerics of their own. Their sum is 59280, itself 4560 thirteens, and neighbour of 59279, or 3487 seventeens (see § § 33—34). And these 59280 years are divided thus: The years to the Flood have 20787, a multiple of three, thirteens and forty-one; the years after the Flood have 38493, a multiple not only of seven and thirteen, but also of nine (it will be remembered that the sum of the 245 Bible years is a multiple of thirteen and nine multiplied by itself four times). The odd years have 28600, or 2200 thirteens; the even years have 30680, or 2360 thirteens.

The birth years among these 41 Genesis years have for their sum 24010, or 7 x 7 x 7 x 2 x 5, with the sum of its factors 28, or 4 sevens. This number has thus 4 features of sevens by itself, Yet it is also neighhour of 1847 thirteens. And more of the like in abundance.

TABLE V.

(The numbers at the left of the events are their order numbers in Table I. As its own order numbers differ therefrom after Number 34, the next seven have theirs given in superior figures).

1	Adam 130, Seth born	[1]130
2	Seth 105, Enosh born	[1]235
3	Enosh 90, Kenan born	[1]325
4	Kenan 70, Mahalaleel born	[1]395
5	Mahalaleel 65, Jared born	[1]460
6	Jared 162, Enoch born	[1]622
7	Enoch 65, Methuselah born	[1]687
8	Methuselah 187, Lamech born	[1]874
9	Adam 930, dies	[2]930
10	Enoch 365, translated	[2]987
11	Seth 912, dies	[2]1042
12	Lamech 182, Noah born	[1]1056
13	Enosh 905, dies	[2]1140
14	Kenan 910, dies	[2]1235
15	Mahalaleel 895, dies	[2]1290
16	Jared 962, dies	[2]1422
17	Flood decreed	1536
18	Noah 500, Japhet born	[1]1556
19	Shem born	[1]1558
20	Lamech 777, dies	[2]1651
21	Methuselah 969, dies. Noah 600. The Flood.	[2]1656
	13 x 13 x 41 x 3	20,787

22	Noah 601, Flood subsides	1657
23	Shem 100, Arphaxad born	[1]1658
24	Arphaxad 35, Shelah born	[1]1693
25	Shelah 30, Eber born	[1]1723
26	Eber 34, Peleg born	[1]1757
27	Peleg 30, Reu born	[1]1787
28	Reu 32, Serug born	[1]1819
29	Serug 30, Nahor born	[1]1849
30	Nahor 29, Terah born	[1]1878
31	Terah 70, Nahor born	[1]1948
32	Peleg dies, age 239	[2]1996
33	Nahor dies, age 148	[2]1997
34	Noah, 950, dies	[2]2006
37[35]	Reu dies, age 239	[2]2026
38[36]	Serug dies, age 230	[2]2049
39[37]	Terah 205, dies	[2]2083
41[38]	Arphaxad dies, aged 438	[2]2096
44[39]	Shelah dies, age 433	[2]2126
47[40]	Shem dies, age 600	[2]2158
50[41]	Eber dies, age 464	[2]2187
	13 x 19 x 2 x 3 x 4 x 10	59280

31. Before leaving the 41 Genesis dates the following is to be noted: Now Bible year 1, the first, is 130; year 245, the last is 4032; year 124, the middle is 3054. The sum of these 3 years is 7216, or 176 forty ones; and the sum of the 3 order numbers is 369, or 9 x 41, the combination of 9 and 41.

Again: The first date in the Old Testament is year 130; the last thereof is 3565, the end of Daniel's first 7 weeks. The first New Testament year is 3916, the death of Anna's husband; the last New Testament year is 4032. The sum of these four years is 11643, neighbour of 11644, or 41 x 4 71, or 284 forty-ones. The reader will perhaps ask, Why the neighbour rather than the number itself? The reason is this: The neighbour 11644 is multiple of 71 as well 41. Accordingly the number 11643 is divided thus: The first Old and New Testament dates 130 and 3916 sum up 4046, twice 7 x 17 x 17; but neighbour of 4047; or 57 seventy-ones. The last Old and New Testament dates have 7597, or 107 seventy-ones. The use of neighbourhood thus makes the design also of 71 where without it only the 41 alone would be possible.

The same junction of 41 and 71 is found in the following: The group of years under 1000, consisting of only three figures, thus being the smallest, begins with year 130 and ends with 987. The largest group of the years with four figures begins with 4011 and ends with 4032. The sum of these 4 years is 9160, or 71 x 43 x 3, the combination of 71 with 43, and the sum of its factors 117. a multiple of both nine and thirteen. Now this sum is thus divided: the two years beginning these groups have 4141, or 41 x 101: itself a multiple of 41, with the sum of its factors 142, or 2 seventy-ones. And the writer might thus go on with forty-ones and seventy-ones for some time.

Now the reason of the appearance of 41 also among the numbers forming the basis for design is this: The number of Bible years 245 is neighbour of 246 or 6 forty-ones.

42. And what is true of Period I having Numerics of its own by itself is equally true of Period II. The sum of its year 40,248 is not only a multiple of 13, 43 and 72, but the sum of its factors 2+2+2+3+3+13+43 is 68, or 4 seventeens. And it is divided thus: Numbers with zeros have 18,486, or those without zeros have 21762, or 13 x 18 x 93: the division being by 18 thirteens, 18 being 2 nines. The one number is combined with seven; the other with 93 or 3 thirty-ones. Now 31 (the reverse of 13) is also frequent in Chronology. Thus the year of the Nativity, 3999 is thrice 31 x 43. The Last Adam is then born. On the other hand the first Adam dies in 930, also a multiple of thrice 31, with 41 as the sum of its factors. Now the sum of these two dates of the death of the first Adam and the birth of the last Adam, 4929, is of course, 159 thirty-ones. But is neighbour 4928 is 7 x 11 x 8 x 8; and its other neighbour 4930, or 290 seventeens. And much more of the like.

And again: The sum 40,248 is divided thus: The years o[the 21 dates of Period 2 occupying places 1, 3, 5, etc. (the places) have 21073 or 1621 thirteens; those occupying the even places have 19175 or 1475 thirteens. The sum of the factors of the first number is 1634, or 38 forty-threes. Those of the second number, 13 5 5 59, sum up 82, or twice 41, with the sum of their figures 28 or 4 sevens.

43. It has already been seen at the end of § 27 that the sum of the years in Period 2 is a multiple of 43 as well as of 13. Accordingly it is divided thus: The births have 22231, or 43 x 11 x 47; and the others have 18017 or 419 forty-threes. These two numbers are moreover both neighbours of multiples

of 13; so that both factors 13 and 43 of the sum 40,248 appear by means of neighbourhood. This division by thirteens is here moreover by twice 9 thirteens; and in the non-birth years it is combined also with seven.

And again: There being in Period 2 just 21 dates or 3 sevens, the three every seventh dates have for their sum 5934, or 138 forty-threes, and the others have 379 forty-threes.

44. Pages more might be continued thus; let one more item be the last for Period 2: Of the 5 centuries covered by it their first and last years are as follows:

$$\begin{array}{c} 1657-1693 \\ 1723-1787 \\ 1819-1878 \\ 1948-1997 \\ 2006-2096 \\ 9153-9451 \end{array}$$

The sum of the years with which these centuries end is 9451, itself 727 thirteens, and neighbour of 556 seventeens. The years with which these centuries begin have for their sum 9153, neighbor of 9152, or 704 thirteens.

And what is true of Periods 1 and 2 is true also of the other periods, though their numerics do not always lie as readily on the surface.

45. As only these 245 individual, years and their sums show these elaborate designs of sevens, thirteens, seventeens, etc., and the change in even a single year will mar the design, and even wholly destroy at least some of its features, we are thus assured that the Designer thus **intended** that only these 245 years make up the true Bible Chronology.

Here indeed the writer's task ends. A few more details are added, however, which explain themselves.

46. The longest interval between the dates in Bible Chronology is from the end of the 49 years of Daniel in 3565 to the death of Anna's husband in 3916. This covers 351 years, itself 13 x 9 x 3, a multiple of 9 and 13. But it is also neighbour of 350, or 50 sevens; and of 352, or 32 elevens: the three prime numbers 7, 11, 13 forming a series. But this is not all: the sum of the two years limiting this interval of 351 years is 7481, neighbour of 7480, 11 x

17 x 2 x 4 x 5, itself a multiple of seventeen, with the sum of its factors, 39, or 3 thirteens, and the sum of their figures 21, or 3 sevens. The other neighbour of 7481 is 7482, or 43 x 29 x 2 x 3, a multiple of 43, with the sum of its factors 77, or 11 sevens: the sum of the figures of 7482 itself being 21, or 3 sevens.

Here then in this single item of the longest interval between Bible dates are duplicated almost all the numeric schemes of Bible Chronology: 7, 13, 17, 43: like the ocean, which is ever reflected in a single drop.

47. This ocean-drop capacity to reflect in a bare fragment the glory of the whole is the characteristic of the God of Revelation as well as of the God of Nature, whose law of Phylotaxis ordained for the leaves of the humblest shrub is found to pervade also the distances of the planets from their sun. And as the movements of the atoms among themselves beholden through the microscope are after the same fashion as the movements of these giants of heaven to be seen through the telescope, so in a single verse of Holy Writ is oft displayed its entire content. When Frederic II of Prussia asked his chaplain to give in one word the evidence for the truth of revealed religion, the prompt answer was: The Jews, Your Majesty. And what the great God has hitherto done in Creation, in History, and in His Book, He has also done in Bible Chronology. It is quite easy to show that in even a tiny fragment thereof is reproduced the vast scheme that pervades the whole. Of this two examples will now be given.

§ 48. Of six persons it is stated that each was 30 at a certain event in his life. Shelab at the birth of his son; Peleg and Serug likewise; Joseph was 30 when he became ruler of Egypt, David when he began to reign: and the Lord at His baptism. This is the only thing recorded of them in common, and thus makes them a class apart. Here are the years when they are 30, and the years of their births and deaths, and the sums of these three items in each case:

Shelah	1723	1693—2126	5542
Peleg	1787	1757—1996	5540
Serug	1849	1819—2049	5717
Joseph	2289	2259—2369	6917
David	2974	2944—3013	8931
The Lord	4029	3999—4032	12060
	14651	14471 15585	44707

The sum of the years when each is 30 is 14,651, or 7 x 7 x 13 x 23. The sum of their birth and death years is 30,056, or 13 x 17 x 17 x 8. In the one the 13 is combined with 7 sevens, in the other with 17 seventeens. The sum of all the 18 years is 44,707, or 181 thirteens times nineteen. With the 23 of 14651 there are here not only the combinations of 13 with 7 and 17, and this doubled in each case, but also the progressive series of the prime factors 13, 17, 19, and 23: Bible Chronology, in miniature.

49. This elaborate numeric design displayed in the years of these 6 persons proves even alone that the Lord **was** 30 in 4029, that He **was** born in 3999, that the Cross **was** in 4032: since every one of these three dates is in the above List. The Ministry, therefore, did **not** extend over 3 years, and the middle of Daniel's week does **not** therefore refer to the Lord's Ministry of three years and a half. And much of the like.

Similarly: David **was** 30 in 2974, **was** born in 2944, **did** die in 3013. 4 Solomon thus is 3017, and 480 and 430 years therefrom back to the Covenant **does** bring to 2107, when Abraham was not 75 but 99. And much more of the like.

50. If the reader will now turn to Table II, page 170, giving the dates for the kings of Judah and Israel, he will there find 9 dates that have this peculiarity: they are the only years for Israel alone. The other 54 dates are for events either of Judah alone, or of Judah and Israel. But these 9, one seventh of the 63 are for Israel alone. They thus form a class by themselves.

They are:			
	6	Omri	3105
	22	Ahab	3133
	1	Ahaziah sole	3134
	28	Jehu	3176
	17	Jehoahaz	3193
	1	Jeroboam joint	3198
	41	Jeroboam joint	3238
	2	Pekahiah	3274
	1	Hoshea	3305
	119		28756

The sum of the regnal years in these nine dates is 119, or seventeen sevens, which the largest and smallest numbers, 1 and 41 have 42, or 6 sevens; leaving for the others 77, or 11 sevens, with the sum of its figures 14, or 2 sevens.

And just as 119 is 7 seventeens, the middle number of the nine is—17.

51. The sum of the 9 years themselves is 28,756, or 7 x 13 x 4 x 79, a multiple of both 7 and 13; with the sum of its factors 103, neighhour of 102, or 6 seventeens; and of 104, or 8 thirteens. The first, last and middle numbers, 3105, 3193 and 3305 have 9603, itself a multiple of 11 nines, but neighhour of 9604, or 7 x 7 x 7 x 7 taken 4 times. Of the regnal years 4 consist of 2 figures: 22, 28, 17, 41. The years opposite them sum up accordingly 12,740, or 7 x 7 x 13 x 4 taken 5 times, leaving for the others 16,016, a multiple of 7 and 13 combined with 11 and the square of 4; the division being not only by 7 thirteens, or 91, but by 4 ninety-ones.

Again: The 8 kings of these 9 dates reigned respectively 12, 22, 2, 28, 17, 41, 2, and 9 years. Their sum is 133: itself 19 sevens, with 7 for the sum of its figures. The first and the last numbers have 21 of this, or three—sevens.

It was noted at the end of the preceding section that the 119 regnal years form 3 groups of sevens. The corresponding groups formed by the years opposite them are:

```
3105—3133
3134—3274
3238—3305
9477   9712   19,189
```

52. The sum of these 6 years is 19,189, with the sum of its figures 28, or 4 sevens. It is itself 619 thirty-ones (thirteen reversed), with the sum of its factors 650, or 50 thirteens. It is neighbour of 19,188 or 13 x 9 x 41 x 4, a combination of 13 with nine and 4 being the special mark of the numerics of the 245 Bible years, with the 41 as a sort of side glance at its other numerics. This sum 19,189 is moreover divided thus: the 3 numbers beginning these groups have 9477, the combination of 13 with 9 nines of 9. Those ending these groups have 9712, neighbour of 9711, again a multiple of 9 and 13.

These 9 dates (the 9 thus accounting for the abundance of nines along with the other numerics here) thus present once more in miniature the same designs running through the Chronology as a whole.

As these 9 dates are of the kings of Israel, and the only thing they have in common is the fact that in these years no event is recorded for Judah, but for Israel only, these Numerics—a design within a design, a wheel within a wheel—thus prove that in Tables I and II the dates of the kings of Israel and Judah are herein properly adjusted to one another; and that the second of the hitherto insoluble problems of Bible Chronology (the other being the Period of the Judges) has been solved.

53. At this point all that remained for the writer to do was to furnish the promised Table VI, and his task was done. But as he was setting up that Table he discovered a slight error in his work. This Table as prepared in manuscript had under the year 3208 the birth of Uzziah and the death of Joash. A comparison, however, with Tables I and II (in the latter a printer's error makes it 4 for 14 Amaziah) showed a discrepancy, as these have the death in the next year. A re-examination of the Scripture passages made it clear that if Amaziah lived after the death of Joash fifteen years (2 Chron. 25: 25), and Amaziah's reign was 29 years, Joash died in 14 Amaziah, rather than 15. This correction affects only the few years of Joash, by pushing them back one year, but does not affect the Numerics except in one particular. But this particular is most instructive withal.

54. If Joash died the year Azariah was born, then Year 3208 has to be marked (^{12}), as both a birth and death year, instead (^{1}) as merely a year. The years marked (^{12}) are thus now: 3013, 3148, 3208, 3272 (see Table I). Their sum is 12,641, neighbour of 12,642, or thrice 7 x 7 x 43. This would of itself suffice to show how even such a slight error in a sub-detail destroys a small design of its own in four years, their only tie being the fact that they are birth **and** death years. But there is more here.

Scripture is clear that Herod died after the Lord's birth. But though the narrative favours only a short stay in Egypt for the holy Family, it does not expressly place Herod's death in the same year. Suppose now Herod did die in 3999, the year of the Lord's birth. Then it is another (^{12}) year, and the sum of these 3 years becomes 16,640, itself a multiple of 5 thirteens and the fourth power of 4, or the square of 16. The sum of its figures is 34, or twice 17. Its one neighbour is a multiple of 7; but its other neighbour is 16641, or 9 **forty-three forty-threes**. 7, 9, 13, 17, and 43 are all here again in the compass of five years, with the Lord's birth year set off by itself, the division being here by 43. The death of Herod is thus demonstrated to be in 3999 as well as the birth of the Lord.

Thus even a slight error on the writer's part is overruled by his gracious Lord to the even greater magnifying of His Word.

55. This work was set up under some physical strain, and about half of it even without manuscript. This double labor of mind and body peculiarly disposes toward error, specially in a work like this which is subject thereto even under the most favourable auspices (In Geden's Greek Concordance to the New Testament which is the best work of its kind, the writer found in less than 2 hours about a hundred errors after a cursory comparison of the earlier portion alone with his own Concordance).

This correction does not disturb the numeric relation of the 126 birth and death years to the 245 years of the List pointed out on page ...... as Feature 22. But the numeric relation between the birth and death years themselves is changed enough to lose Feature 23 and 24.

The writer mentions the presence in his work of this error and the one presently to be spoken of solely as aught due to the reader and to himself. He does not excuse it: the worst excuse is to have one. He grieves over it, and is humbled by it. Magnanimous Joseph could well cheer his brethren with the reflection that even behind their misdeeds the great God had been working for good, but this did not alter the character of their misdeeds.

56. Accordingly the writer has to record to his great regret another error not so slight, the details of which the reader may discover for himself. It in nowise affects a single result obtained in this investigation and exposition. It even leads, as in the first ease, to the discovery of further numeric marvels: namely, that the sum of the 65 order numbers in Table VI, 10,921, has itself 13 for the sum of its figures. But its neighbour 10,920 is 7 x 13 x 2 x 2 x 2 x 3 x 5, with the sum of its factors 34 or 2 seventeens. The other neighbour, 10,922, is 43 x 2 x 127, itself 254 forty-threes, with the sum of its factors 172, or 4 forty-threes: the same 7, 13, 17, and 43, of the ocean in the drop character of the rest. And more of the like.

57. In Table I Year 3133 should be marked (^{2}) as Ahab's death year, and "22 Ahab, dies," should be added thereto. If it were certain that Darius was the one who took Babylon, and received the kingdom the same year, his year 1 should also be marked as a death year, of Belshazzar. But the account in Daniel does not positively necessitate it. Belshazzar was clearly slain on the night of the feast, but Babylon was not necessarily then taken. He may have been slain by his own courtiers for exalting Daniel. And even if Babylon was

taken that night, Darius need not yet, according to this account, have received the kingdom. The conqueror, whoever he was (if not Darius himself), may have been holding the city for him long enough to begin the reign of Darius in the next year. If the feast was toward the year's end, even a short interval would bring Belshazzar''s death and the reign of Darius in different years. It is thus improper to mark 3515 as a death year.

TABLE VI.

The notation for Table VI is as in Table II. The superior figures give the place numbers of the years in this Table, and the numbers following them are their place numbers in Table I. Most of these years are obtainable also from Kings and other books, but some are gotten only from 2 Chronicles, and are marked (*).

YEARS OBTAINABLE FROM 2 CHRONICLES.

[1]	116	Rehoboam born	12: 13	[1]3013
[2]	119	4 Solomon	3: 2	3017
[3]	121	24 Solomon	8: 1	3037
[4]	122	40 Solomon dies	9: 30	[2]3053
[5]	123	1 Rehoboam	9: 31	3054
[6]	124	3 Rehoboam*	11: 17	3056
[7]	125	5 Rehoboam	12: 2	3058
[8]	126	17 Rehoboam	12: 13	3070
[9]	127	1 Abijam, 18 Jeroboam	13: 1	3071
[10]	128	3 Abijam dies	13: 2	[2]3073
[11]	129	1 Asa	14: 1	3074
[12]	132	Jehoshaphat born	20: 31	[1]3080
[13]	133	10 Asa*	14:1	3083
[14]	134	15 Asa*	15: 10	3088
[15]	139	35 Asa, Jehoram born	15: 19	[1]3108
[16]	141	39 Asa*	16: 12	3112
[17]	142	41 Asa dies	16: 13	[2]3114
[18]	143	1 Jehoshaphat	17: 1	3115
[19]	144	3 Jehoshaphat*	17: 7	3117

20	145		Ahaziah born	22: 2	[1]3126
21	152	25	Jehoshaphat dies	22: 31	[2]3139
22	153	1	Jehoram	21: 5	3130
23	154	6	Jehoram sick*	21: 19	3145
24	155	8	Jehoram dies	21: 5 20	[2]3147
25	156	1	Ahaziah dies: Joash born	22: 2 ; 23: 1	[2,1]3148
26	157	1	Attaliah	22: 12	3149
27	158	6	Attaliah dies	22: 12	[2]3154
28	159	1	Joash	23: 1 ; 24: 1	3155
29	160		Amaziah born	25: 1	[1]3170
30	164	39	Joash, Zechariah dies*	24: 22	[2]3193
31	165	40	Joash dies	24: 1	[2]3194
32	166	1	Amaziah	25: 1	3195
33	168	14	Amaziah, Uzziah born, Joash Israel dies	26: 3 ; 25: 25	[1,2]3208
34	170	29	Amaziah dies	25: 1	[2]3223
35	171	1	Azariah	26: 1	3224
36	173		Jotham born	27: 1	[1]3251
37	176		Ahaz born	28: 1	[1]3272
38	179	52	Azariah dies	26: 3	[2]3275
39	180	1	Jotham	27: 1	3276
40	181		Hezekiah born	29: 1	[1]3283
41	182	16	Jotham dies	27: 8	[2]3291
42	183	1	Ahaz	28: 1	3292
43	187	16	Ahaz dies	28: 1	[2]3307
44	188	1	Hezekiah	29: 1, 3	3308
45	192		Manasseh born	33: 1	[1]3325
46	193	29	Hezekiah dies	29: 1	[2]3336
47	194	1	Manasseh	33: 1	3337
48	195		Amon born	33: 21	[1]3370
49	196		Josiah born	34: 1	[1]3386
50	197	55	Manasseh dies	32: 1	[2]3391
51	198	1	Amon	33: 21	3392
52	199	2	Amon dies	33: 21	[2]3393

[53] 200	1	Josiah	34: 1	3394
[54] 201		Jehoiakim born	36: 5	[1]3400
[55] 202	8	Josiah*	34: 3	3401
[56] 203		Jehoahaz born	36: 1	[1]3402
[57] 204	12	Josiah*	34: 3	3405
[58] 206	18	Josiah	34: 8, 19	3411
[59] 207		Zedekiah born	36: 11	[1]3415
[60] 208		Jehoiachin born	36: 9	3418
[61] 209	31	Josiah dies	34: 1	[2]3424
[62] 210	1	Jehoahaz, 1 Jehoiakim	36: 1,5	3425
[63] 216	11	Jehoiakim dies	36: 5	[2]3435
[64] 217	1	Jehoiachin, 1 Zedekiah	36: 9, 11	3436
[65] 224	11	Zedeaih, sons die	36: 11	[2]3446

$$7 \times 10 \times 10 \times 10 \times 10 \times 3 \quad 210{,}000$$

$$(11 \times 17 \times 2123) - 1$$

10,921 67×163 ; neighbour of $(7 \times 13 \times 120) + 1$

and $(43 \times 2 \times 127) - 1$

www.ingramcontent.com/pod-product-compliance
Lightning Source LLC
Chambersburg PA
CBHW071733080526